BROKEN tHINGS

Why We Suffer

M. R. DeHaan

Discovery House®
from Our Daily Bread Ministries

To the thousands of God's patient sufferers,

The Saints

who patiently endure affliction

and whose testimonies of God's faithfulness

have often encouraged and helped me over the hard places,

to the glory of God and the comfort of His saints

CONTENTS

FOREWORD BY MART DEHAAN

My grandfather, M. R. DeHaan, has been at home with the Lord for over forty-five years. Yet the impact of his ministry continues in the lives of men and women who heard him preach and who have read his writings. As one who suffered profound brokenness, M. R. knew what the good news of God's grace meant in his own life. And because God has used the words of this book to challenge and comfort people throughout the world since it was first published, we are pleased to offer it in this new edition.

"If you are being broken, God is working with you. He is making something—something that will someday astound you with its wisdom and beauty. . . . The things we thought were the greatest trials and tragedies we later find to be God's way of bringing us something better. We think broken things are a loss, but God turns them to gain" (M. R. DeHaan, *Broken Things*).

—MART DEHAAN
Senior Advisor of Ministry Content,
Our Daily Bread Ministries
Grand Rapids, Michigan

PUBLISHER'S NOTE

*B*roken Things, written by my father, M. R. DeHaan, is one of the most popular of his many books. This is true, no doubt, because it comforts and encourages those whose lives have been shattered by illness, adversity, and painful losses," wrote Richard DeHaan in his preface to the 1988 edition, one of the first books published by Discovery House Publishers.

The messages in this volume were first broadcast many years ago by Dr. M. R. DeHaan over the Mutual network and independent radio stations at home and abroad. Later they appeared, along with several other sermons, in a hardbound book entitled *Broken Things*. Even after all these years, the book's message is as relevant as ever. Its lessons about suffering are timeless, and the need for a proper perspective on brokenness has not diminished.

This book differs in arrangement from the earlier edition. The first four chapters establish a basic principle in the Word of God that brokenness is a prerequisite to usefulness and service. The next six chapters give some of the reasons for both physical and mental infirmities. The last chapter sets the entire subject of suffering against the background of eternity.

The content of these chapters remains essentially the same as when the messages were preached. A minimum of editing and revision has been done, along with some necessary updating of material. All Scripture passages are from the King James Version.

ONE

THE NEED FOR BROKENNESS

*For thus saith the Lord to the men of Judah and
Jerusalem, Break up your fallow ground, and sow not
among thorns (Jeremiah 4:3).*

Break up your fallow ground." This was
the message the prophet Jeremiah was
commissioned to bring to the people of Israel.
Dark days were settling upon the nation,
and Israel, trusting in her false security, was
permitting the enemy to destroy her because
she was not willing to turn to the Lord. The
people of Israel had longed for ease and
comfort and had permitted their opportunities
and blessings to remain unworked and
undeveloped; therefore the Lord compares their
nation to fallow ground.

Fallow ground is that which is permitted to
lie idle and uncultivated. Instead of producing
grain and fruit, the land becomes covered with
weeds and thorns, and disaster lies ahead.
So the prophet calls to Israel, "Thus said the

Lord . . . Break up your fallow ground, and sow not among thorns."

The spiritual applications of this expression are many and profitable, but the one which comes to mind first of all is that there can be no blessing without effort and no harvest without plowing. Before a thing can be made useful, something must be broken. Before the house is built, the tree must be broken down. Before the foundation can be laid, the rocks must be blasted from their quarry bed where they have long lain in peace and quiet. Before the ripe grain can cover the fields, the soil must be completely broken down. The cutting blade of the plow must turn over the sod, and the sharp teeth of the harrow must pulverize the soil.

Before there can be life, there must be death. Before there can be joy, there must be weeping. The joy that floods the mother's heart at the sound of the first cry of her new newborn babe was preceded by the tears of anguish of childbirth. Our Lord Jesus stated the principle of brokenness in these words: "Except a corn of wheat fall into the ground and die, it abideth alone: but if it die, it bringeth forth much fruit" (John 12:24). This is the law of life in the natural realm, and it is the law of life in the spiritual sphere also. There is no making without breaking.

We are living in a broken world today. As never before, all that seemed permanent and enduring is being broken down; the history of the world is but the breaking of governments, systems, ideals, and programs. The history of every human life, too, is the history of breaking.

What memories come back out of the distant past as one traces again the tedious journey he began years ago! Like misty shadows from the past they take form and materialize again, and he relives the days of sorrow over the broken things of life. The toys he laughed over were broken and cast aside with the stain of childish tears upon them. And then, as he grew older, there were broken promises and broken hopes, shattered dreams, and unfulfilled ideals. Then after marriage he built his home and dreamed of peace and rest, but found that the increase of years increased also the weeping over broken things. All his expectations were shattered in a moment as the little darling in that home was rudely torn from his heart. Perhaps his wife, or his health, or his home, for which he had labored all his life in the anticipation that it would be the scene of quiet last days, were suddenly taken away. Yes, broken things are common life. No one can escape them.

To the child of God, however, every broken thing is but the assurance that God is making something useful. How needful it is for you who today are sorrowing over bitter losses and repining on beds of illness, you whose bodies are broken, to remember that He has said: "And we know that all things work together for good to them that love God, to them who are the called according to his purpose" (Romans 8:28).

If you are being broken by disappointment or bereavement, by loss or pain, by weakness or sickness, remember that although to us broken things are tragedies, to God they are opportunities to be used for His glory. We cast the *broken* things aside and call them "junk," but our God casts the *unbroken* things aside as useless.

BROKEN PITCHERS

To illustrate this truth and bring joy to many of you who today are being broken, we shall call attention to a great number of broken things mentioned in Scripture, showing that only the broken things are useful in God's wonderful dealings with us.

In the seventh chapter of Judges we have the familiar story of Gideon, the sixth judge of the people of Israel after the death of Joshua. Israel was being vexed sorely by repeated attacks of her enemies the Midianites. When the people of God cried to the Lord for deliverance, God raised up a man by the name of Gideon to deliver them. The method of deliverance was unique, for after he had surrounded the camp of the enemy at night, Gideon gave the following instructions:

> When I blow with a trumpet, I and all that are with me, then blow ye the trumpets also on every side of all the camp, and say, The sword of the Lord, and of Gideon. So Gideon, and the hundred men that were with him, came unto the outside of the camp . . . . And the three companies blew the trumpets, and brake the pitchers, and held the lamps in their left hands, and the trumpets in their right hands to blow withal: and they

cried, The sword of the Lord, and of
Gideon (Judges 7:18–20).

With pitchers in their hands, Gideon and his
faithful 300 gained a dramatic and decisive
victory in the routing of the Midianites.

The record is familiar. Gideon was called
of the Lord to go and fight the enemy. Some
32,000 had gathered themselves about him,
but of all these volunteers, only 300 were fit.
With these Gideon surrounded the camp of
the enemy at night. In their hands they held
trumpets and pitchers in which they had
concealed blazing torches. At a command
and signal from their captain, the men were
to break the earthen pitchers and thus let the
light shine forth in the darkness. Then, blowing
the trumpets, they were to give the enemy the
impression that instead of 300 men there were
300 companies of men that had surrounded
them. The effect was stupendous. Fear gripped
the enemy soldiers, and they fled in disorder
throughout the night. The victory was complete.

We are interested in the part the broken
pitchers played in the victory. The pitchers
were earthen vessels, and hidden in them were
flaming torches of light. We who have been

saved are the earthen vessels to whom the Lord has entrusted the blessing of the Holy Spirit and the Word of Life. Within us dwells the Holy Spirit, the omnipotent Holy Spirit of God, the Spirit of Christ, by whom we can do all things. With Him nothing is impossible; for while it is true that without Him we can do nothing, it is equally true that we "can do all things through Christ, who strengtheneth" us. In the pitcher was the torch. The fire and the torch speak of the Spirit of power and victory. Again and again the Holy Spirit, the only source of power and light in the Christian life, is referred to as fire. Fire is one of the many biblical symbols of the Holy Spirit. But this light has been placed in earthen vessels.

Earthen vessels are the symbols of these human bodies of ours. At the wedding at Cana of Galilee, it was into empty vessels that the water was poured and made into wine, the symbol of joy and salvation, at the word of the Lord Jesus. It was in earthen vessels that the widow's small supply of oil was poured until all the vessels were filled. At best we are but earthen vessels to whom have been entrusted the words of life.

In the pitchers were torches. What a picture of the Christian as a result of regeneration! We have been endued with the Holy Spirit, and within every believer dwells this Holy Spirit with all the possibilities and potentialities of Omnipotence. At our disposal is placed the entire realm of Holy Spirit power.

Yet the average believer goes through life without letting that power flow out. It seldom shines forth. Oftentimes there is darkness. So it was in Gideon's day. The torches were there, but there was no light and no victory until the pitchers were broken. Then the light shone forth and the enemy fled in consternation.

How we need to be broken. How often we bewail and bemoan the sad fact of broken lives, but find later that only broken things are used by the Lord, and that only after we are broken are we our very best for God.

There are two possibilities in the Christian life. One is to be in the light, and the other is to walk in the light—to have light within and to let it shine out. The one possibility is life; the other is the life abundant. There is a carnal Christian, and there is a spiritual Christian. We may have, as we read in the fourth chapter of John, the water of life springing up within us; then again, we may have rivers of living water flowing forth out of us, as Jesus said in the seventh chapter of John. Light may be in the pitcher, but the pitcher must be broken if there is to be victory and power.

A BROKEN BODY

"This is my body, which is broken for you" (1 Corinthians 11:24). This quotation by Paul of the words of Jesus at the institution of the Lord's Supper voices a principle which, when properly understood, is of great comfort in times of trial and tribulation. Without the broken body of the Lord Jesus we could not be made whole.

In God's wise counsel everything must be broken before it can be used fruitfully. Jesus expressed this truth when He said, "Except a corn of wheat fall into the ground and die, it abideth alone: but if it die, it bringeth forth much fruit" (John 12:24).

What a world of memory is contained in the words "broken things," which characterizes the journey of life from the cradle to the grave. Even at birth we must be broken away from our mothers; and as we journey down life's pathway, until at last the "silver cord is loosed" and the "pitcher broken at the fountain," our course is strewn with broken things.

From the earliest days of consciousness, man is in a world of broken things. The crying of the infant over a broken toy, the weeping of the child over the broken sled or kite, the sorrow of the young man over a broken trust are common in this world of broken things. There is the broken heart of the mother as the babe she has nursed at her bosom crushes her heart by his waywardness. There is the sorrow of the faithful wife who sits alone in the late hours of the night with broken heart and shattered confidence, waiting for the one she thought loved her.

All along the way lie fragments of things that once were hopes and joys, things that were fashioned into dreams of happiness by the hand of fancy on the wheel of hope. That child who was the dream of all your love breaks your dreams. That business venture you envisioned fails. As the days go by, there are more and more of these broken things; and as the twilight of life comes and the old man totters to the broken sod, he looks back upon a world of broken things.

A BROKEN WORLD

Broken homes, broken hearts, broken bodies, broken hopes, broken health, broken vows, broken lives—what sadness in those words! But this is merely the course of nature. Broken things suggest accidents and calamities. We associate them with disappointments and failure. But all these "tragedies" are known to God, and He can bring out of those broken fragments something far better, more beautiful, more enduring than that precious thing which was broken at our feet.

With the Lord there are no calamities. God knows no disappointments. He knows all things from the beginning, and nothing that happens surprises Him. Knowing everything from the beginning, He has planned that every broken piece in the lives of His own children will fit in somewhere in the complete portrait of His eternal counsel and will.

Are you being broken today upon a bed of illness or by a heart that grieves over the bitterness of a love spurned and abused? Here is comfort for you. God knows all about it, and He would not permit it if He did not see that in the end it will serve a purpose you do not now know.

I long ago learned the lesson—but need to remind myself of it constantly—that God makes only what He breaks and breaks only what He wants to make. If you are being broken, God is working with you. He is making something— something that will someday astound you with its wisdom and beauty. Each time I have passed through the dark vale of disappointment and have cried in agony, "Oh, why, why must this be?" God has always led me out of the gloom into a greater light, out of the straits into a larger place.

Someone has said, "The narrow straits always lead into the wide, wide ocean." The Lord deals with us in that way. Things we thought were the greatest trials and tragedies we later find to be God's way of bringing us something better. We think broken things are a loss, but God turns them to gain. In nature, broken things are cast aside; but in grace, God will never use a man until he is broken.

NATURE AND GRACE

Grace is always the reverse of nature. In the natural realm the first is first, but Jesus says that in the realm of grace the "first shall be last." Nature says that the youngest shall serve the eldest, but grace says, "The older shall serve the younger." Nature says, "He that would be greatest among you, let him lord it over all." But grace says, "He that would be greatest among you, let him minister to the least of these."

If you are being broken by disappointment, by bereavement, by loss, by pain, by sickness, remember that while to us broken things are tragedies and worthless, they are the only things God can use.

The Bible is full of illustrations that support this truth. Again and again God uses broken things to gain the victory. Genesis speaks of a broken fellowship, but God uses it for the exhibition of His grace. Exodus tells of a broken law, but God uses it to prove to man his need of salvation and grace. Numbers depicts a broken covenant. Judges speaks of broken pitchers in the hands of 300 men. Samuel tells of a man with a broken back who sat at the king's table. In the Psalms we read about the outpouring of a broken and contrite heart. In Matthew we read of broken loaves in the hands of Jesus. Mark tells of a broken roof which enabled a paralytic to approach Jesus for healing. In Luke we read of a broken alabaster box; and John tells of a broken home where Lazarus died.

We think of the broken net and the broken
ship, the pieces of which helped to save
Paul and his companions during a storm. We
remember also the broken body of our Lord
on the tree, and we hear Him saying to His
disciples, "This is my body, which is broken for
you."

In each of these examples the breaking was
for a purpose. In every instance a blessing
resulted that so far outshone everything else
that the pain of breaking was soon forgotten.

A BROKEN LAW

Of the many, many broken things mentioned
in the Bible, we want to consider first the
broken law of God. You will remember that after
God had delivered His people out of the land
of Egypt and had led them through the sea into
the wilderness, they came to Mount Sinai. There
God wanted to teach Israel the truth of grace.

It may seem strange when I say that He
gave them the law to teach them the need of
grace, but it is true. There upon the mountain
God gave, by the hand of Moses, two tables of
stone, and on these tables of stone God wrote
the law. Before Moses could bring that law to

the people to whom it was given, however, they had already broken it.

Moses did not break the law when he cast the tables at the foot of the Mount. Israel had already broken it when they desired the golden calf and were dancing about it. Moses' breaking of the stones was a pictorial demonstration of the seriousness of Israel's sin.

ISRAEL MUST DIE

The broken law demands death. The law was never given to save. The law was never meant to take a man to heaven. God knew before He gave the law that there would not be a son of Adam who would ever keep that law. Yea, we may go further and say that God never expected even one sinner to keep that law. It was given by God to reveal the need of grace.

That law was perfect and holy and just. It was the perfect expression of the perfect will of God, and imperfect man could not keep it because it was holy. Sinners could not attain to it. And because it was just, it must condemn everyone who broke it. "The soul that sinneth, it shall die" is the language of the law. "The wages of sin is death," says God's law. "Cursed is every one that continueth not in all things which

are written in the book of the law to do them,"
says the law!

God knew that Israel would break that law.
God expected that they would. He knew the
heart of man far too well to expect that he could
keep His perfect law. He knew that in man—
that is, in his flesh—"dwelleth no good thing."
That law must be broken to convince man that
he needed grace. The breaking of the law by
Israel was the proof and demonstration that "by
the deeds of the law" there should "no flesh
be justified in his sight." Thus the broken law
became the occasion of the revelation of the
grace of God.

THE TABERNACLE

When Moses came down from the mount,
he carried, in addition to the tables of the law,
the pattern of the tabernacle. The tabernacle
is the exhibition of God's grace, just as the
law is the expression of God's justice. The
law knows no mercy. The law demands
punishment for all who break it; and, therefore,
if no more than the law had been given, man
would be forever lost. But God now introduced
the tabernacle—the great type of the Lord
Jesus Christ and redemption by blood.

Every part of the tabernacle spoke of Jesus Christ, but He was symbolized particularly by one article of furniture in the Holy of Holies: the ark of the covenant, the great picture of redemption through Jesus Christ. The ark, which rested in the Holy of Holies, was an oblong box made of wood and overlaid with gold. In the box, together with other articles, was the broken law—not the literal stones Moses broke, but the second tables containing the law that Israel had broken. This law called for judgment and the curse and death. It cried for vengeance. It was the ministration of death.

THE MERCY SEAT

But God made provision for Israel. Even though they had broken the law, they could be saved, for over this broken law in the ark was a mercy seat. Note the following carefully:

Once a year the high priest took blood from the altar in the outer court (a type of the cross of Christ) and carried it into the holiest place. He then solemnly sprinkled that blood on the mercy seat over and above the broken law, which demanded death and judgment and the curse. And then when God, the holy and the just One, came down in the Shekinah cloud of glory in the Holy of Holies, He saw the blood instead of beholding the broken law that demanded the eternal death of the sinner. The blood covered the law.

The law, which demanded blood ("without shedding of blood is no remission"), had been satisfied by that blood. God would not curse His people who were under the blood, for He had said, "When I see the blood, I will pass over you" (Exodus 12:13).

"WHEN I SEE THE BLOOD"

The law was broken by Israel, and what a tragedy it seemed. Yet it was God's way of revealing to His people their need of His grace and the power of the atoning blood. God looked upon the blood and was reconciled. Israel was safe. And God has not changed His method of dealing with sinners. He is still just and holy and must condemn the sinner and punish sin. No man can be saved by the law. The law stands to condemn you. But God has provided another Lamb of atonement whose blood was shed on the cross of Calvary and whose body was broken there to save those who had broken His law.

There is, then, only one place of safety and shelter from the wrath of God, and that is "under the blood." He has said, "Without shedding of blood is no remission."

Yes, the broken law calls for a broken Savior, and the broken Savior calls for a broken heart. Only through things broken can blessing come. Even Jesus could not be a Savior without being broken. God permitted man to break His holy law to convince him of his need for a broken Savior.

ARE YOU BROKEN?

Some of you are being broken today in body, in spirit, and in material things. Remember—until Jesus was broken, He could not be your Savior. That is God's way of doing things. Some of the ingredients of the holy anointing oil in the tabernacle had to be crushed before they were used because until they were crushed their fragrance could not flow forth. For this reason we read: "And thou shalt beat some of it very small, and put of it before the testimony in the tabernacle of the congregation" (Exodus 30:36).

Until the incense was crushed, it could not give forth its fragrance. Until Christ was broken, He could not be our Savior. Except He, the grain of wheat, be broken and ground to flour, He could not be the Bread of Life to us.

Oh, friend, do you realize that only the death of Christ can save you? Only as His body was broken, which means that His blood was allowed to flow out, could He atone for your sin. Without His blood there is no salvation. Are you under the blood? Then you have been redeemed from the curse of the law. But if you are not under the blood, you are still under the curse.

TWO

A BROKEN ROOF AND A BROKEN SHIP

In the second chapter of Mark we read the interesting and instructive story of four men who brought a paralytic to the Lord Jesus Christ by breaking the roof of a house. Jesus was teaching in a home in Capernaum and a great crowd soon assembled until they filled the house. People were crowded around the outside, making it impossible for anyone to get near the door to see and hear Jesus.

In Capernaum was a man who was afflicted with a dreadful disease. He was, humanly speaking, hopeless. He could not walk. He had no means of getting to the Lord Jesus. The other folks had all flocked to hear the Lord Jesus for themselves and had forgotten about the poor man who had no way of enjoying the same blessing.

I fear that in these days there are many similar situations. There are many people who are so busy learning theology and feeding upon the blessed truth of the Lord Jesus Christ that they forget their duty toward sinners round about who have never gazed in faith upon His blessed face.

FOUR MEN AND A SINNER

Can you not see them coming down the dusty road? The afflicted man had no means of getting to the Lord Jesus, but he did have four friends who were interested in him. They made an improvised ambulance, probably similar to a stretcher, and on this the poor fellow lay. But as they came to the house, they found so many folks crowded around the Lord Jesus that there was no room to bring a helpless sinner to Him. What a tragedy! There were so many people who wanted to hear teaching that there was no room for a sinner to come to Christ!

We see similar things in our day. Amid all the divisions and separations among believers, both in and out of the denominations, we are so busy defending the Book and discussing fine points of doctrine that we have forgotten the greatest desire and commission of the Lord Jesus. That this is the correct interpretation is clearly borne out by the fact that Jesus immediately stopped teaching the crowd and applied himself to the more important business of saving and healing this poor paralytic.

Again the story emphasizes the need for our bringing people to Christ if they are ever going to come. The Lord has so ordered the plan of salvation that men and women and boys and girls are saved only as we bring them to Him. Man by nature is not sick. He is dead! He is unable to find Christ without help, as a dead man is unable to come forth from the grave. Because a nobleman came to Jesus in his son's behalf, the boy was healed. Because there was no one to put the paralytic into the pool, he lay helpless for thirty-eight years. Because the friends of Lazarus notified Jesus, showed Him where the tomb was, and took away the stone from the mouth of the sepulcher, Jesus raised the body of Lazarus. Because four men took an interest in this paralytic man, this fellow was saved. Humanly speaking, he would have died in his sin and disease were it not for the interest these four men had in his condition.

God can make a bumper crop of wheat grow on the pavement of Fifth Avenue in New York City without help from man, but He has never done it, and He never will. God's ways of raising a crop of wheat depend upon man. It is only as the farmer plows and drags and sows and cares for his acre that the Lord gives the increase—though He is omnipotent and needs no help from man.

Likewise, in the spiritual realm, God could save every human being without the help of His children, without a tract or a dollar or a missionary. But God does not do things that way. It is God's plan that people will be saved only through the instrumentality of others. His commission is "Go ye, go ye, and preach the gospel." . . . "Faith cometh by hearing, and hearing by the word of God." God has given us the commission and placed at our disposal the only two necessities for soul-winning: the Word and the Holy Spirit. If people are not saved, it will not be His fault; but it may be ours, and ours alone. God has chosen to make the gospel known by people sharing with others the blessed truth of the Word.

In this case of the paralytic man, a broken roof was the only means of getting him to the Lord Jesus. They could not get through the door, and evidently a window was not available. What could they do?

Necessity is the mother of invention, so these men made their way to the roof and began to break through it. Can you imagine the effect on the crowd? Can you not hear a grumbler demand that someone "make those maniacs quit disturbing the meeting"?

It is remarkable that no one succeeded in stopping them from breaking the roof. Perhaps the Lord intervened. Then, the roof was open, and lo and behold, a man on a bed was lowered into the crowd. Can't you hear the hypocrites grumbling some more as they pushed others aside in their haste to keep from getting under that bed?

Notice the conduct of Jesus. Not a word of surprise. Not a rebuke for breaking up a Bible class to save a soul. Not a word because the decorum of the meeting had been disturbed. But Mark tells us, "When Jesus saw their faith, he said unto the sick of the palsy, Son, thy sins be forgiven thee" (Mark 2:5).

Two words need special consideration here: "Their faith." Not the sick man's faith, but *their* faith. I know that men and women are saved by their own personal faith in Jesus Christ and that you cannot be saved by my believing; yet it is also true that men and women may be perishing because we have no faith. It is equally true that people do find Jesus through the faith of others.

It was through the faith of Paul, who dared to trust God, that the gospel came to Europe, and you and I are saved because of Paul's faith. It is was because David Livingston had faith enough to trust God and blaze a gospel trail into the heart of Africa that thousands were saved.

There are some who read this whom God wants on the foreign field, but you do not have enough faith to go. There are some of you who have enough of this world's goods to support a half-dozen missionaries, but because you dare not trust God with what belongs to Him, thousands will slip into eternity without Christ.

O God, make us dead earnest! Set us on fire! Help us to do what needs to be done to bring this paralyzed, dying world to Christ. Many of us have pleasant roofs over our heads. With much labor we have made a comfortable place for ourselves while the world is perishing for lack of Christ. Oh, for a zeal that will make us willing to "tear up the roof" and forget all false propriety and selfish endeavor to bring the message to those who have not heard it!

Think of Christ. It was He who said, "This is my body, which is broken for you." He had a home in heaven, but He left it all and came and dwelt as a man, despised and rejected, a friend of sinners. He went all the way to Calvary to die that you might live.

Here is what is wrong with the church. We have lost our vision of the reality of the terribleness of the condition of lost man. Sin is real! Hell is real! The danger is real! Yet too often we are more concerned about the roof over our heads than the foundation under our feet.

Parents, let me ask you, what is your greatest concern in life? Too often we view with apathy the evidences of unregeneration in our children. We seem so little concerned that our children, whom we love, are on the way to destruction and will spend eternity in hell, where they'll suffer the pangs of the wrath of God because we were more interested in their temporal needs than their spiritual needs. We rejoice over the material prosperity of our children but weep few tears over the fact that they are lost.

O God, help us to break the roof of materialism and worldly interest and open up the house to heaven until the answer comes down! We are not in earnest as we should be. Lord, break our hearts for Thee! Grant us visions of Thy compassion for the souls of men!

A BROKEN SHIP

Paul was a prisoner. He was on his way to Rome to appear before Caesar. A few weeks before, the ship's captain had set sail for Rome against the advice and warning of Paul; and now for two weeks they had been tossed about by the storm. Finally the ship crashed upon the rocks and the waves dashed it to pieces. In the scriptural record of the experience we read,

> "And the rest, some on boards, and some on *broken pieces* of the ship. And so it came to pass that they escaped all safe to land" (Acts 27:44).

No doubt the ship was a very fine vessel. The fact that the sailors dared to set out at that season of the year suggests that it must have been a seaworthy vessel. But no ship of man's building can ever weather the storms of God. Here was a captain and his sailors who trusted their ship. A preacher warned them and said, "Do not go, for a storm is coming." But they did not believe Paul until the ship was dashed in pieces upon the rocks and they were all thrown overboard.

A parallel scene is being enacted every day in every country of the world. Man is trying to build himself a ship to cross the ocean of life and bring him safely to the harbor on the other side. This building is going on everywhere. The various religions of the world testify to man's desire and attempts to build for himself a ship that will carry him safely.

Good works, morality, charity, philanthropy, culture, refinement, honesty, asceticism, fraternalism, politics, and all the rest of the leaky boats of human construction are being tried. Millions and millions of people today are trying to find a Utopia on these ships. But every ship constructed by man must fail.

We read in Acts 27 that when a south wind blew, the boatmen thought all was well and set out. But soon they ran into the storm. There is a storm coming, and every one of our manmade boats will go down. While the sun shines, these ships may seem trustworthy; but when the storm comes, all will fail.

What is your hope of heaven? Are you trusting in a ship of your own building? It will smash to pieces on the rocks by-and-by. Your own life, yea, and works cannot avail. Your righteousness is as filthy rags in God's sight. "Not by works of righteousness which we have done, but according to his mercy he saved us"

(Titus 3:5) . . . "But to him that worketh not, but believeth on him that justifieth the ungodly, his faith is counted for righteousness" (Romans 4:5).

Sinner, have you been broken? All your efforts will never save you. You must abandon your own ship, no matter how much it may cost you or how much you cherish it. It was on broken pieces of the ship that Paul and his companions came to land. When you abandon the old ship of your own merits and cast yourself before God, He will save you. They were not saved by their ship but were saved by the breaking of their ship. If the ship had not been broken, there would have been no pieces; and if there had been no pieces, there would have been no hope.

"Verily, verily, I say unto you, He that heareth my word, and believeth on him that sent me, hath everlasting life, and shall not come into condemnation, but is passed from death unto life" (John 5:24).

THREE

BROKEN LOAVES AND A BROKEN BODY

In the fifteenth chapter of Matthew we have the story of the feeding of the 4,000. For three days the crowds had been following the Lord Jesus in the wilderness and listening to His teaching. Eventually, however, their food supply was gone.

A hungry crowd does not make the best kind of audience for a preacher. A man is more likely to be thinking of his stomach's needs at such a time than of his heart's needs; so the Lord prepared to meet that situation. Of course, He could have given them manna from heaven, as He did with the Israelites; or He could have made loaves of bread grow on the bushes. Instead, Jesus said to His disciples, "You give them to eat."

When the disciples demurred at the seeming impossibility of this, He inquired what they had to eat and found that there were still seven loaves of bread and a few fishes for the disciples and their Lord—enough for their immediate needs, but certainly nothing more. They needed all they had.

Jesus said, "Let me have them." Then, when He had given thanks, He broke the loaves and the fishes and handed them back to the disciples. They in turn passed them to the multitude, and they all did eat and were filled. And when they gathered up the fragments that were left, they had seven baskets full. The bread had increased a hundredfold or more.

This miracle is also a parable. We too are in a wilderness, a dry and thirsty land. This world can never satisfy the human heart. It is not big enough. The heart of man was created for infinity. It was made to be the dwelling place of the infinite God. Only God can fill and satisfy the human heart, and because the human heart was made to embrace Him, nothing less can ever satisfy it. Someone has said that a round world can never fill a triangular heart. There will always be corners that will remain empty. Only the triune God can fill and satisfy the heart of man.

What a hungry world we are living in today! The lust for power, the millions spent in pursuit of pleasure—these are vain attempts to answer the universal cry of the human heart for something that is missing. To this poor, starving, dying world, Jesus says, "I have compassion on them. I will not send them away empty. You give them to eat."

We say, as did the disciples, "Where will we get enough to feed all these?" But Jesus replies, "You have enough. You have enough if you will only share it."

"Why, we have only seven little loaves! We have so little. What can we do?" we say in despair.

Then the Lord Jesus gives us the most sublime truth in the Word: "If you will give Me your little, I will break it up for you and let you give it to others. Then I'll return it to you increased a hundredfold."

Note well the order of events: we give ourselves and what we have to Him; He takes the little and increases it; then we take it to others and are enriched ourselves beyond all imagination. It is not what we have, but what we surrender to Him, that counts. We can never give this poor old starving world a thing until we have first given ourselves to God.

Think of the millions of men and women around the world who have not yet heard the message of the blessed Christ. Faint and hungering in the wilderness of this world, they are turning to pleasure and debauchery and false religions to quiet that yearning for something that will satisfy. Hear their cry!

The world is full of quacks who offer to give these suffering souls nostrums and patent medicines to relieve their ills, but they only make the hunger deeper, the throat more parched, and the heart more empty. Others attempt to satisfy the heart with the social gospel, good works, philanthropy, education, philosophy, and travel; yet the cry goes up, "Give us to eat!" And we are the only ones who have anything permanent to give these starving souls.

When Christians are willing to place in the hands of the Lord the little they have, He will do great and marvelous things.

BROKEN LOAVES

The loaves belonged to the disciples until Jesus needed them. Will you give your loaves to Him? You have a life, but it is not your life only; Jesus is asking for it. Will you let Him have it and break it up and feed it to a dying multitude?

You have hoped to give your life to a prosperous career in business or in the professions. You have an education. You are ready to make good. The world offers you success and money, popularity and pleasure. But Jesus asks for your life. He wants to use it in the ministry, or on the foreign field, or somewhere else. But such service and surrender means the breaking up of ideals, plans, and dreams.

Jesus says of your life, "Let Me have it."

"What will I have for myself?" you ask.

Jesus gives the answer. "If you will be ready to give your all for those who are dying, I will take care of you. Give your bread to those whom I died to save, and I will take care of you."

Hallelujah! I have found it so. I have eaten from the seven baskets which were left over after I placed my all on the altar for Christ and left a profitable medical practice for the toughest job on earth—the task of preaching the gospel.

Broken loaves! The loaves of your life, your talents, your education, your ideals! Say, "Here they are, Lord Jesus!"

God has given some of you several golden loaves. He has blessed you with wealth and material things. You thanked God as you nibbled their sweetness. You praised Him as you buttered that bread while millions of others were starving for the Bread of Life. Oh, you may have thanked God for giving you the loaves, but have you heard His call to give them to others? "Give, and it shall be given unto you; good measure, pressed down, and shaken together, and running over, shall men give into your bosom. For with the same measure that ye mete withal it shall be measured to you again" (Luke 6:38).

God is asking only that we entrust to His hand the few loaves we have and let them be broken. Let us be broken—broken to a vision of the need of lost souls. We confess that we believe a man is lost without Christ and goes to an eternal hell. We talk about it, write about it— and then, tragically, do so little about it.

God is asking for broken loaves, for broken hearts, for broken men and women—broken from their selfishness, broken from their indifference, broken from their covetousness, broken from their lethargy, and awakened to the profitableness and glory of being out and out with God. Let Him have whatever you have. Say with the hymnwriter,

> O Cross that liftest up my head,
> I dare not ask to fly from Thee;

I lay in dust life's glory dead,
And from the ground there blossoms red
Life that shall endless be.

A BROKEN BODY

"This is my body, which is broken for you"
(1 Corinthians 11:24). Thus did the Lord Jesus
speak of His death when He took the bread
and broke it before His disciples. He never
asks us to do something He has not done. If
what we have been speaking of in these pages
seems hard—too hard—one look at Calvary
should stop all complaining. There the Son of
God hung on the cross as the sin-bearer of the
world.

Broken things are the result of sin. If sin had
not entered, our world would not be broken as it
is. There would have been no broken promises,
no broken laws, no broken trusts, no broken
hearts and homes and hopes, no broken bodies
and spirits and dreams, no bleeding wounds.

But the broken things may be overruled and
made to glorify the wisdom of God because He
sent His Son to be broken, that all these might
be healed. Nineteen hundred years ago He
came and began a work of redemption that was
potentially finished when He died on Calvary,

but awaits the consummation when He shall put all things under His feet and make all things new.

His body was broken literally also—broken when they scourged Him and the skin burst open and the raw flesh stood out, broken when they crowned Him with thorns and the cruel barbs sank into His blessed brow, broken when they drove the cruel nails through His blessed hands and feet and impaled Him on a tree, broken when they pierced His side and the water and the blood came forth to testify to the reality of His suffering as well as His death— broken for us.

I can see Him standing there with the bread in His hands as He said to those at the table, "This is my body, which is broken for you." Now He asks only that we be broken for Him; that we break these earthen pitchers and let His light shine. The apostle voices this truth: "I beseech you therefore, brethren, by the mercies of God, that ye present your bodies a living sacrifice, holy, acceptable unto God" (Romans 12:1).

Our Savior asks that we give to Him our few loaves and fishes so that He may increase them for us and give them back to us to give to others. We cannot escape His command: "Go ye into all the world, and preach the gospel to every creature" (Mark 16:15).

He asks that we break up the roofs that we have carefully constructed for our own pleasure and turn things upside down in our zeal to bring lost men and women to Christ.

He asks that we learn the lesson of the broken net and trust Him fully.

He asks that you, sinner, abandon the ship of your own righteousness and throw yourself on the cross where Jesus was broken for you. If Paul's fellow voyagers had stayed on the ship, they would all have been lost. Their salvation lay in their leaving the ship.

We cannot be His until we are broken of self, and we cannot be instruments fit for God's use until our hearts have been broken by penitence and our lives by suffering. Claim the comfort of His promise, the promise that cannot be broken: "In the world ye shall have tribulation: but be of good cheer; I have overcome the world" (John 16:33).

> Many are the afflictions of the righteous; but the Lord delivereth him out of them all (Psalm 34:19).

FOUR

A BROKEN VASE

As we study the broken things of the Bible, each becomes more precious and beautiful. The fourteenth chapter of Mark tells of a broken alabaster box of ointment poured out upon the blessed head of our Lord Jesus.

"And being in Bethany in the house of Simon the leper, as he [Jesus] sat at meat, there came a woman having an alabaster box of ointment of spikenard very precious; and she brake the box, and poured it on his head" (Mark 14:3).

A great deal of conjecture has attended these words, and no definite answer can be given as to the exact identity of the women mentioned in the passage. Some say that she was Mary of Bethany, the same woman who anointed the Lord Jesus in the incident described in the twelfth chapter of John. Others point out that this can hardly be so because the account in John tells us that Jesus was entertained in the home of Lazarus, whereas Mark's record speaks of Jesus in the house of Simon the leper. Others say that this Mary was the sinful woman who had been so marvelously saved from a life of sin by the Lord Jesus (John 8:1–11). We shall not dogmatize. Enough that the Holy Spirit does not give her name in this passage before us. If we suppose that she was a sinful woman who had been forgiven by the Lord, we shall not fall short of the mark.

There is an interpretation which tells us that this precious vase of ointment was a cosmetic used by the women in Jesus' day, especially by those women who sought to beautify themselves for baser purposes. To suppose that this is true only makes the narrative more instructive.

Here is a woman who had been living a life of sin. She resorted to the age-old and yet modern scheme of adorning and perfuming herself to cover her corruption so that she might more easily entrap her victims. But then a man named Jesus crossed her path. Before He left her, she had been saved and cleansed by His power, and her bitter life of sin and shame had been changed into a song of eternal gladness. Virtue replaced vice; glory replaced shame.

Now, her one desire was to give to her Savior the devotion she had once given to her life of sin. So she broke her precious ointment, that which she had used in days past for her sinful purposes, and poured it upon the head of her Redeemer. What a lesson for us! Many of us remember how we served the world in days gone by. We held nothing back. We served the devil with all our might. No hours were too late, no expense too great, no sacrifice too costly. We were willing to spend and be spent for the sinful, fleeting pleasures of the world. Many a costly vase of ointment was lavished upon ourselves or our sinful friends. But since Jesus came into our lives, how things have changed. We still possess those same powers and abilities we gave to the devil, but our time and our education and our talents can no longer be used for the world.

Have we broken the alabaster box and poured it over His head with the same lavish abandon and liberality that we sacrificed to the world? Consider the use of your time. Do you remember that before your conversion you could sit until one o'clock in the morning at the card table, or spend hours at the bowling alley? But now if the church service lasts a bit too long you complain. How we shouted at games and parties, but how seldom do we send a note of praise to God!

Do you remember the money you spent for pleasure and worldly amusements? Not nickels and dimes, but bills—fives and twenties and even more in one evening. Now, though that alabaster box is as full of money as before, you merely take the lid off and let the Lord have a smell of it, while you carefully keep the rest for yourself. While missions are pleading and begging, you are carefully sealing the alabaster box. How I wish I could make all born-again believers as liberal for the cause of the Lord as they were for the devil before they were saved!

The alabaster box must be broken. Nothing less will do. Now there are several things this woman could have done, and I suppose everyone in the house would have thought her action splendid. She could have taken off the cover of the box and poured a teaspoonful of the ointment upon His head, or she could have emptied all the ointment upon His head and kept the bottle so that she could fill it again and anoint herself. But she did not. She broke the vase. She destroyed every possibility that anyone else would be anointed with the contents of that bottle.

Do you see the meaning of the act? The box could be broken only once. It was an act of consecration that was final as far as the woman's yielding herself to Jesus was concerned. How many there are whose lives resemble the broken alabaster box! It is true of most men and women of God who have really been used of the Lord that somewhere in their lives there was a crisis, a test in which they were broken. And they can date from that day a new inflow of power and outflow of service.

I am convinced that the great need of Christians today is a breaking of the vase once and for all. I am not thinking of a second blessing nor a second definite work of grace. Grace is something God does. I am speaking of something you do when you yield yourself and lie broken at His feet.

The woman broke the vase. Here was a woman who refused to be hampered by tradition. To my knowledge, such a thing had never been done. It was without precedent, but she dared to be different.

We have been carrying on our church work in the same traditional, musty way for so long that anyone who dares to depart from the moss-covered methods of the past is considered a novice or an upstart fanatic. But history reveals that progress comes when someone is willing to be different. When George Whitefield went outdoors to preach because no building was big enough, he was ridiculed for his "foolishness." How could he expect a blessing outdoors? Unheard of! Unreasonable! The church—that was considered the place of blessing. But Whitefield went, and God blessed, and one of the mightiest revivals swept the world.

Dare to be different! Dare to be a fool for Christ's sake!

The woman broke the vase. We have already anticipated that it was a final act. But it had even further significance. The woman wanted to let it be known that this act was for Christ exclusively, without thought of self or anyone else. Martha served, but not exclusively for Him. It was in His honor, but it was for others, too. Simon entertained our Lord, but others were included. But what this woman did was for Christ alone.

What is much of our service these days? Is it for Him or for something or someone else? Imagine if you can the Lord Jesus himself standing before you, His hands outstretched and pierced with nails. See what He did for you?

What have you done for Him that can begin to compare with what He did for you? "Oh," you may say, "I have worshiped Him in God's house." Yes, but that was for your profit too. "Well, but I pray." Yes, for things you need. "I read His Word." Yes, and that is profitable to you. Do you ever sing just to please Him? Do you teach Sunday school because you seek to do something for Him? Is it a passion for others or love for Him that prompts your service? Do you serve as an officer because you are interested in the church, or because you want to help the pastor? Or do you do it for Him?

I sometimes wonder whether I have ever done anything just for Him. When I look at Him, everything I have done seems so small, so negative. Nothing I could possibly do or sacrifice or give could ever compare with what He has done for me.

I do not expect all of you to feel as I do regarding my debt to my Savior, for perhaps you do not owe Him as much as I do. Perhaps you have not sinned as I have, and you have not had so much forgiven. But I know that I could never repay Him for what He has done for me.

FIVE

WHY WE SUFFER

The greatest sermons I have ever heard were not preached from pulpits but from sickbeds. The greatest, deepest truths of God's Word have often been revealed, not by those who preached as a result of their seminary preparation and education, but by those humble souls who have gone through the seminary of affliction and have learned experientially the deep things of the ways of God.

The most cheerful people I have met, with few exceptions, have been those who had the least sunshine and the most pain and suffering in their lives. The most grateful people I have met were not those who had traveled a pathway of roses all their lives through, but those who were confined, because of circumstances, to their homes—often to their beds. They had learned to depend upon God as only such Christians know how to do.

The "gripers," on the other hand, are usually those who enjoy excellent health. The complainers are those who have the least to complain about. But those dear saints of God who have refreshed my heart again and again as they preached from sickbed-pulpits have been the men and women who have been the most cheerful and the most grateful for the blessings of almighty God.

The Bible tells us distinctly that there is a special reward and a special crown which the Lord has prepared and laid up for those who suffer patiently. This principle is suggested by the incident recorded in 1 Samuel 30.

David, along with four hundred strong, healthy men, had gone out to seek the enemy. Two hundred, however, had remained behind because they were weary and faint, probably because of some physical infirmity. These David had left behind to guard the camp and the equipment of those who went into the heat of the battle. After the victory had been won, the four hundred who had been active participants in the battle refused to share with those who had remained behind and said, "We'll give them just a little bit, but we're going to take the spoils."

At this point David stated the eternal principle in the words of 1 Samuel 30:24: "As his part is that goeth down to the battle, so shall his part be that tarrieth by the stuff: they shall part alike."

Those of you who remain by the stuff are not overlooked or forgotten by God: there is a very definite and special reward laid up for God's patient sufferers.

If you, child of God, are upon a bed of illness, if you are being troubled by pain or discouragement, remember that God will always use our suffering for His purposes. Our suffering silences Satan, our suffering enables us to glorify God, our suffering makes us more like Christ, our suffering makes us appreciative, and, ultimately, our suffering teaches us to depend on God.

SUFFERING SILENCES SATAN

God uses the experience of His children to silence the enemy of the Word of God and the Lord Jesus Christ. Probably the best example of this is the story of the patriarch Job. Remember that Job was a wealthy man, but he was also a spiritual and godly man. When the Lord called Satan's attention to the fact that Job was a godly man who feared the Lord perfectly with all his heart, the devil accused Job of doing it only for the gain and profit which came to him materially as a result of his fearing the Lord.

You will recall that God gave Satan the privilege, the right, to lay his hand upon Job and to take away his possessions and his family. The result was that Satan was silenced; for Job, instead of murmuring and complaining and turning in bitterness against almighty God, praised the Lord and was able to say, "The Lord gave, and the Lord has taken away; blessed be the name of the Lord."

Is it not wonderful to think that God is willing to use us to silence the adversary, the devil, by the testing and the trials and the tribulations which come upon us? Many times I have stood at the bedsides of God's patient sufferers and have seen the enemy silenced—he who would say that we serve God only in sunshine. Many times I have stood at the bedsides of those racked with pain for years and seen smiles of gratitude and praise to God—smiles unlike any other from those who have been trained in the school of affliction.

If you are one of God's "Satan-silencers," praise Him for it.

SUFFERING ENABLES US TO GLORIFY GOD

In the eleventh chapter of John's gospel we find another reason the Lord permits calamity, trouble, pain, suffering, and sorrow to come upon His people. There we find the record of the death of Lazarus, a dear and precious friend of the Lord Jesus Christ.

The Savior knew that Lazarus was sick. He could have healed him at a distance, but He permitted Lazarus to die in order that He might reveal a blessed truth that could not in any other way be taught to Lazarus and his two sisters and His followers. Therefore the Lord Jesus Christ, in the course of His conversation with His disciples, says, "This sickness is not unto death, but for the glory of God, that the Son of God might be glorified thereby" (John 11:4).

The next verse tells us: "Now Jesus loved Martha, and her sister, and Lazarus" (11:5). Yet our Lord permitted Lazarus to die in order that He might be glorified, and that His friends might experience the joy of resurrection.

SUFFERING MAKES US MORE LIKE CHRIST

The third reason God permits His children to suffer is that He can accomplish in this way the ultimate purpose for which He himself has called and chosen us. The purpose of God in choosing and saving a man or a woman is to make that person more like the Lord Jesus Christ himself.

The Lord is not interested merely in saving you, keeping you out of hell, and taking you to heaven when you die. His purpose is much wider and deeper than providing salvation merely as a means of escaping punishment and entering into bliss at the end of life. We read in Romans 8:29: "For whom he did foreknow, he also did predestinate to be conformed to the image of his Son, that he might be the firstborn among many brethren."

This is a precious truth from the Word of God. Those whom He foreknew were all in God's plan from eternity. He predestined you not primarily to be saved from hell, or to go to heaven when you die, but to be conformed to the image of His Son.

Now, if it is the purpose of the Lord ultimately to make us like the Lord Jesus Christ, that means there must be suffering, pain, and sorrow in our lives. No believer will ever be like Christ without these afflictions, similar to those which Christ experienced so deeply.

In the epistle to the Hebrews we read concerning the Lord Jesus Christ: "For it became him, for whom are all things, and by whom are all things, in bringing many sons unto glory, to make the captain of their salvation perfect through sufferings" (Hebrews 2:10). And in the closing verse of that same chapter we read: "For in that he himself hath suffered being tempted, he is able to succour them that are tempted" (2:18).

To be made like the Lord Jesus Christ implies that we follow Him in all things. This means not only the Mount of Transfiguration, but also the garden of Gethsemane and the hill of Calvary; it means darkness and suffering. That is why Paul could say in Philippians 3:10: "That I may know him, and the power of his resurrection, and the fellowship of his sufferings, being made conformable unto his death."

O to be like the Lord Jesus Christ! We often sing:

> Earthly pleasures vainly call me,
> I would be like Jesus.
> Nothing worldly shall enthrall me,
> I would be like Jesus.
> Be like Jesus, this my song,

In the home and in the throng,
Be like Jesus all day long,
I would be like Jesus.

And if we would be like Him, certainly then we must be willing to follow Him wherever He leads.

SUFFERING MAKES US APPRECIATIVE

Another reason for God's testing and trials is that they make us more appreciative of the blessings God bestows upon us. True, it is often more difficult to praise God when darkness besets us than when the sun is shining brightly, and yet it is also true that often we do not appreciate our blessings until they take flight.

Among these innumerable blessings that come to us when God sets us aside in His providence and in the wonderful provision He has made according to Romans 8:28—namely, "that all things work together for good to them that love God, to them who are the called according to his purpose"—we have this also: suffering gives us a sense of appreciation that we can obtain in no other way.

SUFFERING TEACHES US
TO DEPEND ON GOD

Another reason the Lord allows the suffering and the pain which so often try us is that we may learn to depend upon Him and not rely upon our own strength.

When the children of Israel found themselves in difficulties, instead of turning to the Lord, they turned to an alliance with the nations around them, particularly the Egyptians. The Lord told them that their strength was not in the nations or in their army. But, He said to them, "In returning and rest shall ye be saved; in quietness and in confidence shall be your strength" (Isaiah 30:15).

How many of you during your days of health felt that you were indispensable in your work or in your home or your business? You were convinced that if anything happened to you, everything would go wrong. You had to be there. You couldn't take time off from anything to be quiet. You rushed and fretted and hurried around, and then the Lord permitted you to be laid aside. Your business, your family and loved ones, and your work had to get along without you. And you found out—to your surprise— that they got along as well without you as with you. Yes, you found that when that day came, God was able to guide and direct and see you through experiences you thought you could never endure.

I must confess that I had to learn that difficult but great lesson. Such education is hard on our pride. It humbles us. It takes something out of us, and yet it teaches us that we must learn to depend upon the Lord. We read in Exodus 14:13 that when the Israelites stood before the sea with the Egyptians behind them and deserts and mountains on each side, the Lord said, "Stand still, and see the salvation of the Lord."

Oh, the precious lesson He teaches us when we learn that God can undertake for us and do things far beyond our comprehension! The Bible says: "Not by might, nor by power, but by my Spirit, saith the Lord of hosts" (Zechariah 4:6).

Are you one of God's shut-ins? Did you have to learn some of these difficult lessons? Ah, then your life has been enriched, and I know that even now you can praise God for His wonderful dealings.

SIX

IN SUFFERING WE EXERCISE FAITH

But he knoweth the way that I take: when he hath tried me, I shall come forth as gold (Job 23:10).

It is said that a bar of steel worth $5 when made into ordinary horseshoes will be worth only $10. If this same $5 bar is manufactured into needles, the value rises to $350, but if it is made into delicate springs for expensive watches, it will be worth $250,000. This original bar of steel is made more valuable by being cut to its proper size, passed through the heat again and again, hammered and manipulated, beaten and pounded, finished and polished, until it is finally ready for its delicate task. In similar fashion, the farmer does not spend time tilling the sand hill that has no value for crops; he puts most of his work and time into the heavy field which has the greatest promise of an abundant harvest.

These examples set forth a vital truth concerning the child of God. Let us realize that God expends His effort only on that which gives promise of having value. When God leaves us utterly alone and does not visit us with difficulties and testings and trials, we may be sure that our lives are barren. Someone has said, "Sunshine all the time only makes a desert." We need the clouds, the dark days, the storms, and the rain just as much as we need the sunshine. And God, who is molding our lives, seeking to make us like the Lord Jesus Christ, knows what is best for us.

In the verse that we quoted at the beginning of this chapter, we hear Job saying: "But he knoweth the way that I take: when he hath tried me, I shall come forth as gold" (Job 23:10). Notice that Job does not say, "I know the way that He takes," but rather, "He knoweth the way that I take."

We would like to know what God is doing. We would like to pull aside the veil and see the end from the beginning. We would like to know the way that He is taking. But if we did, and if we could see, we would not need faith to believe and to accept God's way.

So Job, in the midst of all his deep afflictions, found comfort, not in the fact that he knew the reason and the answer for all of God's dealing with him, but in the truth that God knew what He was doing. "He knoweth the way that I take," he said confidently, and then his faith leaped over every barrier; and as he looked into the distant future, he cried, "When he hath tried me, I shall come forth as gold."

Probably we experience one of the most trying means by which God accomplishes His purpose in our lives when we are forced to sit still. When our hearts yearn to do something for Him, when we would like to be active and out in the world witnessing for Christ, when we long to do something important, probably even spectacular, then the Lord places us in a position of inactivity and causes us to learn the lesson of quietness and stillness.

That, I believe, is one of the greatest tests of a Christian's faith. Yet, as we pointed out in the previous chapter, those who remain behind with the stuff are as important as those who are found in the front lines of the battle. David said, "As his part is who goeth down to the battle, so shall his part be that tarrieth by the baggage."

In the previous chapter we indicated a few results of trials and testings in the life of a Christian. In this chapter we shall consider a few more of the lessons that only trouble and trial and persecution can teach us. The Word tells us, "For we are saved by hope: but hope that is seen is not hope: for what a man seeth, why doth he yet hope for? But if we hope for that which we see not, then do we with patience wait for it" (Romans 8:24–25).

God wants to strengthen our faith. Only exercise can give strength. We know how true this is in the physical realm. We must use our bodies and our muscles as well as our minds if they are to grow. The same is true of our faith. The faith that is not exercised is a faith that will not grow; a faith that is not tried will never be strong. Faith is believing what we cannot see and understand. According to Scripture, "faith is the substance of things hoped for, the evidence of things not seen."

The very fact that we cannot understand why God deals with us in the way He does exercises our faith. If we could understand all of God's dealings, we would not need faith. I need no faith to see a tree when my eyes are open or to hear the birds when my hearing is good, but to believe the things we cannot see and cannot understand and cannot fathom—that is faith. We exercise faith when we accept the promise of almighty God.

If you are suffering in some way and you have been asking, "Why must I suffer? Why cannot I be like others?" then remember that God says, "All things work together for good to them that love God, to them who are the called according to his purpose." That is God's promise. You may not understand why, but when you receive and accept His Word, and when you believe that what God sends to you is the best for you, then you may claim this assurance with the hymnwriter:

> I do not know why oft 'round me,
> My hopes all shattered seem to be;
> God's perfect plan I cannot see,
> But someday I'll understand.
>
> Someday He'll make it plain to me,
> Someday when I His face shall see;
> Someday from tears I shall be free,
> For someday I shall understand.

Another purpose in God's dealing with us is to purify our lives and to make us more like the

Lord Jesus Christ. "Beloved, think it not strange concerning the fiery trial which is to try you, as though some strange thing happened unto you: But rejoice, inasmuch as ye are partakers of Christ's sufferings; that, when his glory shall be revealed, ye may be glad also with exceeding joy" (1 Peter 4:12–13).

This tells us that we are to rejoice in the hope and the confidence that God's purpose is being accomplished in our lives.

SUFFERING TEACHES US PATIENCE

We have already touched on the fact that the Bible tells us that God has prepared a special reward for those who suffer patiently (see chapter 5). But patience can be learned only by enduring.

"And hope maketh not ashamed; because the love of God is shed abroad in our hearts by the Holy Ghost which is given unto us" (Romans 5:5). That verse follows upon another verse: "But we glory in tribulation also" (Romans 5:3).

I want you to notice that Paul was able to say, because he had advanced far in Christian experience, that we glory in tribulations also. It is not always easy to do this, and yet Paul could say it. Now notice why Paul was able to glory in tribulation: "Knowing that tribulation worketh patience; And patience, experience; and experience, hope: And hope maketh not ashamed . . ." (Romans 5:3–5).

Patience can be learned only by enduring. Unless our patience, like our faith, is tried, we will never learn to be patient. Therefore, among the many, many blessed lessons and results of our tribulations and troubles and trials is this: We learn to be patient.

SUFFERING MAKES US SYMPATHETIC

"Blessed be God, even the Father of our Lord Jesus Christ, the Father of mercies, and the God of all comfort; Who comforteth us in all our tribulation, that we may be able to comfort them which are in any trouble, by the comfort wherewith we ourselves are comforted of God. For as the sufferings of Christ abound in us, so our consolation also aboundeth by Christ. And whether we be afflicted, it is for your consolation and salvation, which is effectual in the enduring of the same sufferings which we also suffer: or whether we be comforted, it is for your consolation and salvation" (2 Corinthians 1:3–6).

Anyone who has felt the chastening hand of the Lord as He sought to mold and shape his life knows the truth of the statement that one can never be sympathetic toward others until he has needed sympathy himself. The world knows little about true Christian sympathy, about entering into the sufferings of others. And it is a fact that until we have suffered ourselves, we are, as Job says, "miserable comforters."

The people who can bring the greatest comfort and peace into our hearts are those who can speak and minister to us out of their own personal experience. That is true not only of physical suffering but of our spiritual life also.

Those of us who seek to serve the Lord Jesus Christ can soon tell when we meet other Christians whether they have had a vital experience with the Savior. With such Christians we are able to fellowship. We talk the same language. The minutes and the hours fly by, and we feel refreshed and comforted as we exchange our experiences concerning the Lord Jesus Christ.

The same is true of physical illness. Those who have been used of God to comfort us most, to speak intelligently and understandingly in a way that brings comfort and peace and relaxation, are those who themselves have passed through the valley of testing and know whereof they speak. During the illnesses and the days and the months that I have been permitted to be laid aside from the active ministry, a great many of my friends came to visit. All of them, I believe, were sincere and earnest and well-meaning. They came with the intention of lifting the load and brightening the way and extending their sympathy. Yet as I look back upon those experiences, I can divide all of these friends into just two classes: those who helped me and those who hindered me.

I am not saying this as harsh criticism, but as an expression of truth. There were those who did their very best, but they didn't know what I had endured; they didn't know what I had experienced. They knew nothing of my pain and suffering and heartache and temptations. And so although they sought to say something that might comfort me, after they were gone, I had to say with Job of old, "Miserable comforters are they all."

But, ah, how sweet, how precious, how helpful was the ministry of those who came and, though they did not talk as much, by the very press of their hand and by relating their

own experiences showed me immediately
that they knew what they were talking about.
How wonderful it is to learn sympathy through
suffering!

Before we close this chapter we must stop
and think of Him who is the greatest sympathizer
of all, the Lord Jesus Christ. There is One who
can sympathize with us in our sufferings because
there is not an experience in our lives about
which He does not know. Every valley that we
are called upon to pass through, He has passed
through ahead of us. He knew what it was to
be poor. He knew what it was to be forsaken by
friends and left alone. He knew what it was to be
thirsty and to be weary. He knew what it was to
have enemies revile Him. He knew what it was to
spend sleepless nights as He wrestled in prayer
for those who did not appreciate Him.

Jesus knew what it was to be tempted and
yet to be victorious. He knew what it was to
suffer pain as Roman soldiers hung Him upon
the cruel cross of Calvary and drove the nails
through His precious hands and His precious
feet until He cried out, "My God, my God,
why hast thou forsaken me?" He knew what it
meant to go through the valley of the shadow,
to taste death for every man and woman. He

knew what it was to have the curse of the law
with all its blackness and threatening rest upon
Him because He bore another's sin. Therefore,
today, He is able to help those who are
tempted. There is not a thing that is not known
to Him.

"For it became him, for whom are all things,
and by whom are all things, in bringing many
sons unto glory, to make the captain of their
salvation perfect through sufferings. . . . For in
that he himself hath suffered being tempted,
he is able to succour them that are tempted"
(Hebrews 2:10, 18).

O suffering, weary one, look now to the Lord
Jesus Christ and receive His comfort!

SEVEN

MAKING US
WHAT WE OUGHT TO BE

In considering the ministry of suffering, we must remember one primary, basic principle: "whom the Lord loveth He chasteneth" (Hebrews 12:6). If we belong to Christ, we may expect that He is going to take an interest in our welfare; and since His purpose is to make us like himself and to bring out in every believer the highest in fruitfulness and service, He expends much labor upon us so that we may become what He desires. In Romans 8 we find these words: "And we know that all things work together for good to them that love God, to them who are the called according to his purpose. For whom he did foreknow, he also did predestinate to be conformed to the image of his Son, that he might be the firstborn among many brethren" (Romans 8:28–29). I have quoted verses 28 and 29 because I believe they are inseparable. God has placed them together. Most Christians are familiar with Romans 8:28.

However, Romans 8:28 without the next verse is incomplete. Romans 8:28 tells us that all things work together for good to those who love God, but the following verse gives the reason God expends His work and labor upon us. Those whom He did foreknow He predestinated to become like His Son, Jesus Christ. When we realize how unlike Christ most of us are, we begin to recognize the necessity of much work in order to accomplish this purpose.

In Psalm 84:11 God says that He will not withhold any good thing "from them that walk uprightly" before Him. If in the providence of God it is best for us to have trouble and tribulation, we must believe that a loving God will not withhold suffering in order to make us what we ought to be.

Remember, the normal path of the believer is one of tribulation. Jesus said, "In this world ye shall have tribulation." And Paul tells us that we must "through much tribulation enter into the kingdom."

So, we may consider this truth as a basic rule: If we do not suffer trouble and tribulation and persecution, it is either because we do not belong to the Lord or because we are lacking in fruit and service. Let us never forget, "whom the Lord loveth he chasteneth."

In past chapters we have seen some of the purposes for which God permits or sends upon us troubles and tribulation—to silence the devil, to glorify God, to make us more like Jesus, to strengthen our faith, to purify our lives, to teach us patience, to make us sympathetic, and to separate us from the world. In this chapter I want to add a few more reasons, although I realize that the list is inexhaustible. The benefits derived from being chastened by the Lord are many and varied. However, there is one we must not fail to mention.

SUFFERING MAKES US AND KEEPS US HUMBLE

God wants His children humble. It was pride that caused Satan to sin; it was pride that caused our first parents to fall. God hates pride. He exalts the humble. And so one of the reasons God places us in the fires of tribulation and testing is that we may learn the most important and indispensable lesson of Christian growth: humility.

Probably the best expression of this to be found in Scripture is the example of the apostle Paul. From his writings we notice that he was afflicted with a physical malady, which he called a "thorn in the flesh." Many have speculated about the nature of this malady. Some have supposed that Paul was afflicted with ophthalmia as a result of the blinding vision on the day of his conversion. Others believe he was hunchbacked; some say he had a speech impediment; still others suggest that Paul was afflicted with malaria. We are not going to spend time trying to determine which of these is correct. Rather, we are interested in why the Lord permitted this faithful servant of His to suffer throughout the days of his life with this "thorn in the flesh."

In Paul's own account in 2 Corinthians 12 he tells us that at a certain point in his Christian experience he had been caught up into paradise, into the third heaven. There he had received directly from God a revelation that had not been made known to any other.

Now, this was a wonderful experience. But Paul, who was the last to claim perfection and who realized that in him—that is, in his flesh— there dwelt no good thing, knew that such an experience might easily be perverted to become the basis of vainglory and fleshly pride.

So he tells us: "And lest I should be exalted above measure through the abundance of the revelations, there was given to me a thorn in the flesh, the messenger of Satan to buffet me, lest I should be exalted above measure. For this thing I besought the Lord thrice, that it might depart from me. And he [that is, the Lord] said unto me, My grace is sufficient for thee: for my strength is made perfect in weakness. Most gladly therefore will I rather glory in my infirmities, that the power of Christ may rest upon me. Therefore, I take pleasure in infirmities, in reproaches, in necessities, in persecutions, in distresses for Christ's sake: for when I am weak, then am I strong" (2 Corinthians 12:7–10).

Paul received the definite assurance from the Lord that his "thorn in the flesh" had been given so that he might not become proud and puffed up but would remain humble. If he were to lose his humility, God could no longer use him.

Perhaps we can apply this truth to our own hearts and lives. Possibly the Lord does not allow us the relief that we pray for because He knows that to grant the request would only be detrimental to us. As believers we must remember that God always answers prayer, but He does not always answer with a "Yes." Sometimes, in His infinite wisdom, His answer is "No" because He knows what is best for us.

I want to press this point home to those of you who are suffering and have been asking why God does not answer your prayers for healing and restoration. God does answer your prayers. But He probably has not answered them in the way that you wanted. Possibly you have not prayed in His will; you have not made your prayer the prayer of the Savior, "Father, if it be thy will, let this cup pass from me." Our prayers must be in the will of God, for the simple reason that God knows better than we what is good for us.

Let me illustrate. Early in my Christian ministry I was called to apprehend a man who was behaving irrationally and violently. After we had captured him in a field, we found that he carried a loaded revolver. I returned it to his wife, but she said, "I don't want that gun. You'd better keep it, Doctor. I don't want to see it anymore." So I took the gun, together with some of the bullets, and placed it in one of the drawers of my desk and promptly forgot about it.

Then one day my son, Richard, a lad of about five, was rummaging through my study and came upon this revolver and the bullets lying near it. I remember vividly how he came running to me with the revolver in one hand and the bullets in the other hand. Looking up at me, he said, "Daddy, look what I found! May I have this? May I have this?" Now, of course, you who are parents know what I did. Quick as a flash, I took it away from him, after looking to see whether any bullets had been placed in the magazine. Then I took the bullets away from the boy and said, "No, no, Richard, you cannot have that gun. It's too dangerous for you."

Did my son understand? He did not! He began to cry and plead and beg. There was nothing in all the world he wanted that day more than that beautiful pistol. Nothing else counted. That was the one thing he felt he could not do without. He must have it. But because I was a loving father, and even though he did not understand, I refused his petition. Now that he has grown up, he knows that the best thing for him at that time, even though it caused him pain, was my firm refusal and my answer "No."

Christian friend, are we not like that? We are only children in the faith. We are so limited in our understanding and in our reasoning, but we have a heavenly Father who knows what is best for us. Ofttimes we come to Him and plead and pray and petition for something we think we cannot do without. Yet He says firmly and tenderly, "No, my child, I must refuse this petition. I cannot let you have this thing that you feel you need more than everything else in your life." Although we cannot understand now, I assure you that by-and-by when we meet Him face to face and reach full maturity as children of God, we shall understand.

SUFFERING TEACHES US TO PRAY

And speaking of prayers and petitions, I am sure that thousands of you will agree when I say that we never learn to pray—really pray—until we are in a place where there is nothing left to do but pray. As long as we can help ourselves, we often neglect the ministry of prayer. But when there is nothing left to do, how effectively we can pray!

The greatest people of prayer I have ever known were the greatest sufferers. And the greatest strength in my ministry is the ministry of the thousands who can do little more than pray and write, "We are praying for you."

SUFFERING BRINGS REWARDS

There are many results of the ministry of suffering, but one I want to touch on in closing is this: There is a special reward for those who suffer. There are rewards for Christian service, for soul-winning, and for looking for the coming of Christ; but the Lord has set aside a special crown—a special reward—for those who will suffer patiently for Him. Paul tells us, "If we suffer, we shall also reign with him" (2 Timothy 2:12).

There is a special place of service and reigning and power and authority in the kingdom for those who have been the Lord's patient sufferers here below. Peter wrote, "Beloved, think it not strange concerning the fiery trial which is to try you, as though some strange thing happened unto you: but rejoice, inasmuch as ye are partakers of Christ's sufferings; that, when his glory shall be revealed, ye may be glad also with exceeding joy" (1 Peter 4:12–13). And in Hebrews 2:10 we are told that Christ was made perfect through suffering.

Someone has aptly said, "Steel is iron plus fire. Soil is rock plus crushing. Linen is flax plus the comb that separates and the flail that pounds and the shuttle that weaves." And the

Christian life, if we are to be what God wants us to be, is faith plus suffering. It is God's way of doing things. It is God's own way of making us what we ought to be. God's way is through fire, and through the fire He will perfect us.

EIGHT

WHY ART THOU CAST DOWN?

Why art thou cast down, O my soul?
And why art thou disquieted within me? Hope thou
in God: for I shall yet praise him, who is the health of
my countenance, and my God
(Psalm 42:11).

The "cast down" believer is an abnormal believer. The happy and rejoicing Christian is the normal Christian. The gloomy Christian is abnormal in that he has not yet learned the proper perspective of life and has not yet learned to interpret and translate all the trials and afflictions of life in terms of future glory and reward. But while the normal Christian is the happy Christian, it is also true that the average Christian is not normal. Sad to say, many believers, while they should be happy, are like David in Psalm 42, cast down and complaining bitterly because of their afflictions and trials.

Surely there are no people on earth who should be as happy and rejoicing as those who have been redeemed by the precious blood of the Lord Jesus. The Bible says that all things are ours, and someday we shall be heirs of the earth and inherit all things. We can afford to wait and be patient, for after a little while He who said He would come will come, and we shall reign with Him over and upon the earth.

ALL THINGS ARE OURS

In the Lord Jesus Christ every believer has a treasure that cannot be described in terms of material wealth and possessions. We are members of the wealthiest and happiest family in all the universe, for God is our Father. He is the Creator of all things. The gold and the silver and the cattle on a thousand hills are His. He is the Father of every believer, and we are heirs of all things that are His.

The Son is ours and we are His. The Lord Jesus Christ gave His life and shed His blood upon Calvary's cross. He broke the bands of death and arose, and today He is seated at the right hand of God the Father in heaven. Soon He is coming again to put down all rule and authority and power and to reign upon this earth in perfect righteousness and justice. And we shall reign with Him.

The Holy Spirit is ours—He who came on the day of Pentecost to indwell every believer. To think that this blessed Holy Spirit, one of the infinite eternal persons of the Trinity, should dwell within our bodies and make them His temples is beyond all comprehension.

Salvation is ours; sanctification is ours; glorification is ours. All the promises of the Book are ours. We wait for that glad day when Jesus will come and we shall receive new bodies like the body of our Lord; painless, deathless, sinless bodies in which we shall be able to enjoy to the full all the blessings of the new heaven and the new earth forever and ever. There will be no more weariness, sickness, pain, sorrow, parting, dying, or sinning; but through all eternity, on and on, forever and ever, we shall enjoy in infinite capacity the "things which God hath prepared for them that love him."

WE SHOULD BE HAPPY

Yes, indeed, when Christians stop to think what they are by grace and what lies ahead, they should be inexpressibly happy. But sad to say, this is not always true. Too often, like David, we must cry out, "Why art thou cast down, O my soul? And why art thou disquieted within me?"

The experience of David is the experience of all of us at some time or another, but we are not alone in these experiences. As we study the saints of the Scriptures, we find that this was the common experience of all. Although we have everything in the world for which to be thankful, it remains a fact that we are still in these frail mortal bodies of ours and are compelled to cope and struggle with the problems of time and material interests.

As we study the Book, we find that even the greatest heroes of the faith had their moments of darkness and despair. When they took their eyes off the Lord and the eternal implications of their present trials, they too cried out, "Why art thou cast down, O my soul?"

This was true of Abraham when he fled the land of Canaan when the Lord sent the famine. Instead of trusting the Lord, he went into Egypt—with tragic results. Moses had his discouraging moments, and Elijah, after his victory over the prophets of Baal, allowed an evil queen, Jezebel, to send him into a depression so that he desired to die. Despair came also to the prophets Jonah and

Jeremiah, and even John the Baptist had his dark moments. And we could multiply these examples, including King David.

DAVID IN THE VALLEY

In Psalm 42, David, the man of many moods, found himself once more in the valley of gloom and despondency. He cried out, "Why art thou cast down, O my soul? and why art thou disquieted within me?" As he looked out upon the world through his dark glasses, it seemed to David that there was no hope.

Hear him as he complains to God: "Lord, how are they increased that trouble me! many are they that rise up against me. Many there be which say of my soul, There is no help for him in God" (Psalm 3:1–2).

At times it seems that God is deaf, and that the heavens are made of brass, but this is never the fault of God or His promises. And in an effort to help those of you who are downcast and discouraged and have had your minds filled with misgivings and doubts, let me bring you both a diagnosis and a treatment. As a spiritual physician, I shall first diagnose the disease of soul despondency, and then by His grace administer the remedy of the Word of God.

THE CAUSE OF DESPONDENCY

To arrive at the proper diagnosis of our human despondencies, we must bear in mind certain facts. The first is that we are still in the flesh, and even though we are saved, we still have to contend with bodies that are subject to all sorts of infirmities. Add to this the fact that we also have souls that are subject to varying emotions and are highly sensitive to changing circumstances. They are influenced even by the condition of our bodies, as I shall try to point out.

Although we are justified in the spirit the moment we believe and receive Christ, our souls need continual sanctification, and our bodies must await complete redemption and glorification at the coming of our Savior. These being facts, we must reckon with them and take them into account. As long as we are here, we must contend with these old bodies of ours, and we cannot escape this struggle.

THE DIAGNOSIS

First among the causes of gloom and depression is the natural disposition with which some people come into the world and which they carry with them to their grave. This does not mean that there is no victory over this condition, but merely states a fact that all people, even Christians, are not born with the same cheerful disposition and ability to look on the bright side of life. Some people are born bowed down, and they go to their grave bowed down. They are of a naturally gloomy disposition through no fault of their own. The world may blame them and call them pessimists, but God, who knows all things, takes into consideration their inherited disposition. Along with such hereditary traits, some people encounter unfortunate circumstances in early life; as a result, their natures become twisted, and they acquire a cynical attitude toward life.

As a result of the multiplication of these factors, such persons look at life through dark glasses. Things that may look pink and rosy to another are dismal to them. When such a person is born again, God places within that believer a new nature. And while that new nature will never change the old, incorrigible, corrupt nature, it will, however, put down and keep in subjection and gain the victory over that old nature. But the old remains the old. "That which is born of the flesh is flesh" and always will be flesh.

After a man is saved, he still has the old nature and the old disposition to contend with; however, he does not contend in his own strength but in the strength of the new nature and the indwelling Holy Spirit. This is a point that must be constantly borne in mind. Every new man is two men—the old and the new. The old still has all the old characteristics and weaknesses, whereas the new is created in perfect holiness and sinlessness. The Bible abounds with examples of this. The fiery prophet Elijah, even after his tremendous victory over the prophets of Baal, was still subject to his old despondency and wanted to die.

The same was true of Peter. Peter was the hasty, trigger-finger type, ready to blow off at a moment's notice. After he was saved, he still remained the impetuous Peter and needed the rebuke of Jesus, and even later, the severe public rebuke of Paul.

Thomas was a doubter before his conversion, but after he was saved he was still the old Thomas, even though he was a new man. After the Resurrection, he still refused to believe until he had seen the evidences of the nail and spear wounds in the resurrected Jesus.

Am I addressing these words to someone who is included in this category? Perhaps you too are a gloomy Christian. Somehow things always look dark to you, and you cannot help seeing the serious side of every circumstance. I am not endorsing such an attitude. On the contrary, I want to show you how you may have victory over it.

Remember that the Lord understands and takes into consideration the fact that you must struggle with a disposition that makes victory doubly difficult; but you can have victory if you will face the issue squarely and remember that God's promises are more dependable than your own feelings.

PHYSICAL INFIRMITIES

A second cause of despondency is physical weakness or illness. Our souls and our bodies are inseparably related, and the feelings of our souls are intimately dependent upon the conditions of our bodies. It is in the spirit that our victory lies, both over the disposition of our souls and the infirmities of our bodies. An aching, suffering body affects our soul, our feelings, and our outlook on life.

Frequently people go to the preacher imagining that they have a spiritual problem when the trouble is entirely physical and a doctor could give them more help. In my experience in the practice of medicine, I have seen hundreds of cases where supposedly spiritual problems were actually the result of some physical disease or infirmity.

The reverse is also true. Many Christians are suffering from weakness and sickness that no doctor can cure because these afflictions are God's chastening upon them for spiritual disobedience or unconfessed sin.

I do not want to be misunderstood. I do not mean for one moment to imply that all weaknesses and sicknesses among Christians are the result of unconfessed sin. I am sure that such cases are in the minority. But it is true that some sicknesses and diseases among believers are the result of God's chastening for unconfessed sin.

Paul leaves no doubt in this matter. He wrote to the believers at Corinth:"For this cause many are weak and sickly among you, and many sleep" (1 Corinthians 11:30).

The apostle is speaking of believers who refuse to judge sin in their lives and who will not examine themselves, particularly in the light of the teaching concerning the Lord's Supper. Paul says that when the believer knows there is a sin in his life and refuses to put it away by confession and repentance, it may become necessary for the Lord to take a hand in his or her cleansing. He does this by sending sickness and weakness upon that person; and if the person persists in disobedience and unwillingness to repent, He may even take him home by way of death.

Therefore, we ought to examine ourselves in the light of God's Word and put away all known sin. No Christian can be happy when he knows he is out of the will of the Lord.

In the next chapter we shall continue our diagnosis of the disease of Christian despondency and consider some of the mental and spiritual causes of believers being cast down. Then we shall give you the remedy as revealed in the Word of God by the Great Physician himself.

Are you cast down today? Do you have to cry out with David, "Why art thou cast down, O my soul? And why art thou disquieted within me?" Then do this: examine your own heart and see if the trouble lies in your own life. Is there a spirit of disobedience and rebellion? Is there sin in your life? If so, take God's remedy: "If we confess our sins, he is faithful and just to forgive us our sins, and to cleanse us from all unrighteousness" (1 John 1:9). Then claim the promises of God and remember that your salvation depends upon *His* word—not *your* feelings.

NINE

GOD'S PATTERN
IN OUR LIVES

David was in the deep valley of despair when he wrote Psalm 42. As he looked about him and saw the wicked prospering and the righteous suffering, he was at a loss to know the meaning of it all, and his heart was despondent. He spent his time weeping and lamenting, as we read in verse 3, "My tears have been my meat day and night, while they continually say unto me, Where is thy God?" (Psalm 42:3).

David could not understand God's mysterious dealings. He had searched his heart; he remembered how he had served the Lord. Yet he found himself in the deepest distress. To David it seemed that the Lord was fast asleep and utterly oblivious and indifferent to his sad state and his deep depression. In Psalm 44 he cried, "Awake, why sleepest thou, O Lord? arise, cast us not off for ever. Wherefore hidest thou thy face, and forgettest our affliction and our oppression? For our soul is bowed down to the dust: our belly cleaveth unto the earth. Arise for our help, and redeem us for thy mercies' sake" (Psalm 44:23–26).

David was surely in a bad way. Everything seemed dark. His prayers apparently were unanswered, and it seemed as if his great God had fallen asleep and was deliberately hiding His face from him. What evil thoughts Satan places in our minds when we get our eyes on our troubles and off the Lord and His wise providence!

Then, to make matters worse, the enemy began to taunt David and said, "Where is your God? Where is the God in whom you boasted and rejoiced? Where is He whom you praised so loudly a few days ago? Now here you sit, a child of the God whom you worship, and you moan and groan and cry and weep and complain and are in despair."

David was about to abandon all hope—and then he achieved the proper perspective. He realized what caused his depression and turned to God as the only cure for his trouble and difficulty.

MANY CAUSES OF DEPRESSION

In the previous chapter we pointed out a few reasons for the depression of spirit Christians often experience. We are not merely spirit, even after we are saved. We still have souls and bodies. The body is heir to all sorts of human weakness and pain and suffering, while the soul is subject to varying and changing emotions and feelings, and these often affect our spiritual outlook. As I have said, we must recognize the fact that until we receive our redeemed bodies, we have to cope with the weakness of the flesh and the temptations of the soul.

I pointed out that many of God's children are depressed and cast down because of their naturally gloomy dispositions. Some have happy, carefree dispositions; others are always conscious of life's serious side. In order to have victory, these dispositions must be made subject to the new nature. There are also physical weaknesses that tremendously affect our spiritual outlook and our joy of soul.

It is a great deal easier to be happy and to praise God when all is bright and prosperous. When things are going fine, it is easy to praise the Lord. I hear some pious soul say, "We should always be happy, even when things are bad." I quite agree that we should; but the fact remains that it is much easier to praise the Lord when we are healthy than when we are racked with pain and burning with fever.

Many times people have come to me with spiritual complaints and deep depression that were actually caused by some physical malady or sickness. They needed the advice of a doctor more than the counsel of a preacher. I remember one case in particular. A dear saint of God found herself in the deepest valley of despair because she imagined she had committed the sin against the Holy Spirit. She was driven almost to insanity. She traveled from preacher to preacher seeking relief, but the darkness only deepened.

When she came to me, I was led to suggest that she go to a physician instead and find out if there was not some physical cause of her mental depression. Upon examination it was found that she was gradually being poisoned by badly infected teeth. A dentist removed the teeth, and within three weeks her depression was gone, and she was again the happy Christian she had been formerly.

I do not recommend tooth extraction for all cases of mental and spiritual depression, but

I merely want to emphasize the fact that the condition of our bodies affects our souls and our outlook on life. It is foolish to ignore this.

One man who suffered from a spiritual depression so deep that he wanted to die was thoroughly cured by a good meal. This man, you may recall, was Elijah. He was so dejected that he lay down under a juniper tree and asked the Lord to let him die. But the Lord said, "Elijah, all you need is a good meal and a long nap and you will be all right."

God prepared a good meal, Elijah had a good sleep, and then he got up and went in the strength of it forty days. He lived to be a mighty prophet who served the Lord for many years. The man who wanted to die never died, for he was translated into heaven.

MENTAL DISEASES

What is true of physical weakness is true also of mental illness. There is no question that many of the maladies of spirit from which God's dear children suffer are in their heads, not their hearts. Certain mental diseases are accompanied by depression and despair. However, it is also true that at times our troubles are truly of a spiritual nature. Much of this

distress is due to ignorance concerning God's
plan for our lives, ignorance of the promises of
God, failure to confess our sins, and selfishness
in our prayers.

First, let me again emphasize that
unconfessed sin can cause doubt and spiritual
depression. If there is sin in the Christian's life,
there cannot be joy and victory. Perhaps that
sin is nothing more than failure to believe and
appropriate the promises of God.

A distorted concept of God's love and grace
also may cause spiritual gloom and despair.
There are thousands of people whose lives are
one sad dirge of gloom and doubt because they
have been taught that the plan of salvation is
more difficult than it is. They think they must do
something to be saved—live perfect lives, keep
the law, work, toil, and worry. One day, when
they have lived in comparative victory, they are
happy. The next, when they have failed, they
moan and cry that they are lost again. They
dwell only upon those isolated texts in Scripture
that have no application to their lives at all.

Two things must be kept in mind. First,
salvation is all of grace and does not depend in
the least upon our goodness, works, religion,
success, or keeping the law. Second, God has

also made a provision that when saved people fail, they can receive cleansing and forgiveness through simple confession: "If we confess our sins, he is faithful and just to forgive us our sins and to cleanse us from all unrighteousness" (1 John 1:9).

BEREAVEMENT AND SORROW

Another common cause of gloom is bereavement and sorrow. Let me repeat that it is much easier to rejoice in the Lord when your family is well than when you sit beside the sickbed or even the casket of one who is dear to you. That is the time the devil taunts you and points to others who live in sin and wickedness and never seem to have any trials or troubles. And he says, "You! Are you a child of God? If there is a God in heaven, why does He permit these things?"

Asaph also had that experience. Hear him in Psalm 73:

> But as for me, my feet were almost
> gone; my steps had well nigh slipped.
> For I was envious at the foolish, when
> I saw the prosperity of the wicked.
> For there are no bands in their death:

but their strength is firm . . . Their
eyes stand out with fatness: they
have more than heart could wish . . .
And they say, How doth God know?
and is there knowledge in the Most
High?

   Behold, these are the ungodly, who
prosper in the world; they increase
in riches. Verily, I have cleansed my
heart in vain, and washed my hands
in innocency. For all the day long have
I been plagued, and chastened every
morning (Psalm 73:2–4, 7, 11–14).

Here, indeed, was a problem, and when
Asaph considered how the wicked prospered
and the righteous suffered, he cried out in
despair: "When I thought to know this, it was
too painful for me" (Psalm 73:16).

But now notice his following words:

Until I went into the sanctuary of God;
then understood I their end. Surely,
thou didst set them in slippery places: thou castedst them down into
destruction . . .

For, lo, they that are far from thee
shall perish: thou hast destroyed all
them that go a whoring from thee.

But it is good for me to draw near
to God: I have put my trust in the
Lord God, that I may declare all thy
works (Psalm 73:17–18, 27–28).

Note that word "until." Until Asaph looked
beyond the present, he was unable to see that
the wicked were doomed to punishment and
that God was dealing with His own child in love,
preparing him for a glory that could come only
through suffering and pain.

When we interpret our troubles in terms of
the future and eternity, then all is bright. How
much better to suffer for a little while as a
child of God than to be cast into an eternal hell
forever as a sinner! God does not chasten those
who are not His. He lets them go. There is only
judgment and hell for them at the end of the
road. But He is constantly working to make you
who are His ready for the glory.

Remember, Paul said, "For our light affliction,
which is but for a moment, worketh for us
a far more exceeding and eternal weight of
glory; While we look not at the things which

are seen, but at the things which are not seen:
for the things which are seen are temporal;
but the things which are not seen are eternal"
(2 Corinthians 4:17–18).

Yes, God is working out a pattern in our
lives. In this pattern there are bright spots and
dark backgrounds, all of them necessary for
the complete portrait. As we pass through
the dark experiences of life, however, we see
only that dark piece. We see only the present
and the immediate, but God sees the whole
picture of our life as it will appear when the last
stroke of the brush has been completed. Our
experiences also resemble a jigsaw puzzle.
Here is a black piece that seems to fit nowhere
at all. It does not make sense. Here is a little
brighter piece. But by-and-by the Master will
take all the pieces that look so disconnected
to us now and will carefully arrange each piece
in its proper place. Then we shall find that the
dark pieces of the puzzle were as important to
the completion of the full beauty of the pattern
as the bright sections. Then we shall see His
completed work—the work of a Master who
makes no mistakes.

Take heart, dear child of God. Your Father
makes no mistakes. He loves you more than

you love Him, and even as the child cannot understand the rod of an earthly father until he reaches maturity, so, too, we cannot understand all now. But someday we shall understand. "Now we see through a glass darkly, but then we shall see His face clearly. Now we see only the separate parts and pieces, but then we shall know it in its perfectness, even as He knows now" (1 Corinthians 13:12, my translation).

TEN

HE WILL NOT FAIL US NOW

In the world ye shall have tribulation; but be of good cheer; I have overcome the world," said Jesus to His disciples. Until the Christian faces this fact, he will never be able to have the victory of faith that overcomes the world. Just as surely as God saves you, He also begins a good work in you which will never cease until He has accomplished His purpose of making you like His Son, Jesus Christ.

Our Father does not always explain why He allows us to pass through many dark experiences. He wants us to develop and exercise our faith, without which it is impossible to please God.

David's complaint in Psalm 42 was a bitter one. When he looked upon the wicked and saw how they prospered and how God's people seemed always to be tested and tried, he came to the point of despair. But when he sat down soberly with the Word of God and came to that

place of complete submission to God's will,
he could rejoice even in tribulation. And that is
the victory, which is the only cure for spiritual
depression and gloom.

I have tried in the previous chapters to point
out that our feelings are very much dependent
upon many things. Our circumstances, our
environment, our natural disposition, our
physical and mental health, and the struggle
we have with the flesh all have a bearing upon
our feelings and our outlook upon life. They
often cause us to cry out, "Why art thou cast
down, O my soul?" But thanks be to God, the
Great Physician is equal to them all. He has
the remedy and He never fails. So after having
diagnosed the case, we shall attempt in this
chapter to show you the cure.

In David's psalms we find five well-defined
steps. If followed, they will bring the same
joy and victory David experienced and then
recorded for all the generations of suffering and
despairing ones in all ages.

1. Remember God's faithfulness. At first,
David remembered the wrong thing. In Psalm
42:4, he said, "When I remember these
things, I pour out my soul in me." But he
was remembering his troubles, his tears and

suffering, and the taunts of the wicked. And the more he thought on his own trouble, the worse he felt. But after his third cry of "Why art thou cast down?" in Psalm 43:5, there was a change in David:

> We have heard with our ears, O God, our fathers have told us, what work thou didst in their days, in times of old. How thou didst drive out the heathen with thy hand, and plantedst them; how thou didst afflict the people, and cast them out.
>
> For they got not the land in possession by their own sword, neither did their own arm save them: but thy right hand, and thine arm, and the light of thy countenance, because thou hadst a favor unto them (Psalm 44:1–3).

Yes, David remembered that God had never failed his forefathers in days of old. Many were their dark days and experiences, but in the end God was always faithful. David must have also remembered what he had written in Psalm 34, when he was on the mountaintop and not in the valley of despair: "Many are the afflictions of the righteous: but the Lord delivereth him out of them all" (Psalm 34:19).

This, my friend, is the first thing you must do. Stop and think back. Has God ever failed? Oh, yes, the days have been dark, but in the end has He ever failed? I know what your answer is. Well, then, He will not fail you now. In the end you will see the glory of the Lord through your deepest afflictions. Remember, and when you do, you will be ashamed that you ever doubted Him at all.

2. Read the Word. Go to the Scriptures. David could only remember what God had done in the past by turning to the record of the Word of the Lord. And as he read the record of God's faithfulness, his soul was restored.

May I suggest that much of the gloom and despair of Christians in every age is because they have been too occupied with their troubles and have neglected the precious promises of the Word. Among the thousands of victorious sufferers I have been privileged to know in my ministry, I have found that a knowledge of the Word and victory in trial and suffering are inseparably associated. I have seen patient sufferers who had lain in pain upon beds of illness for years and yet radiated joy and happiness and perfect peace because they appropriated the precious promises of God.

I do not doubt for one moment that the Lord sometimes places us upon our backs so that we may have more time to study His Word. Many of us are too busy when we are well to give proper attention to the study of His Word. And then the Lord lays us aside so that we will have time for this most important and indispensable need in our Christian lives.

3. *Pray.* No Christian can grow without much prayer. I say much prayer. The habitual, perfunctory prayers we offer on set occasions—in the morning, at evening, and at mealtime—are commendable, but if they are the extent of our prayer life, we will be spiritually impoverished.

Many Christians have been laid aside for just one reason: that God might teach them the importance of prayer. Many of us, and that includes myself, never really learned to cry out to God in deep earnestness until we were put in a corner where we could do nothing else.

God's sufferers have always been the best pray-ers. All over the world the Lord has thousands of saints whom He has laid aside in their homes and upon their beds because they are effective pray-ers. Sometimes we wonder why God does not raise up these precious saints who lay upon beds year after year. Perhaps because it would mean an irreparable loss to the entire church of Jesus Christ.

I could not preach were it not for that great army of prayer warriors, many of whom God permits to remain behind with the stuff in order that they may pray. If they were well, their time for prayer might be limited because of their many other duties; but their prayers are needed—yea, they are indispensable—and so while others carry the burden in the public, active service, the faithful laid-aside ones carry the burden in the private but equally active chamber of prayer.

4. Have faith and hope. Notice how the complaint of David ends. He says: "Hope in God; for I shall yet praise him, who is the health of my countenance, and my God" (Psalm 43:5).

He declares, in effect, "My hope is in God, for I know that I shall yet praise Him. This trouble may be severe, but it is only for a moment. It will not last, and someday the sun is going to break through again."

I like the homely philosophy of the preacher who said, "My favorite text in the Bible is: 'It came to pass.' I like that text, and it gives me so much comfort. 'It came to pass.' Yes, all my troubles come to pass. They won't last. When I am sick I say, 'It came to pass.' When I am in trouble, 'It came to pass.'" That may be a simple philosophy, but it is effective.

In our lives, too, these things come to pass; but more than that, they are for a definite purpose. God does not permit even one thing to happen to us without a divine and wise purpose, which we shall know by-and-by.

The hope of the future is the cure for every ill of the Christian. It is not for us to unravel the mystery now; it is enough to know that He doeth all things well and that "all things work together for good to them that love God."

To the world it may seem that it does not pay to serve the Lord. And even to us the way may often be dark, and we cannot see how these present experiences can be of value. But we are to judge all things in the light of His coming and giving of rewards. Paul says, "Therefore judge nothing before the time, until the Lord come, who both will bring to light the hidden things of darkness, and will make manifest the counsels of the hearts: and then shall every man have praise of God" (1 Corinthians 4:5).

This is a precious truth. There is a time of reckoning coming, and then we shall all receive from His hand the rewards based upon all the circumstances of life. Man judges by the outward appearance, but God will judge not only our deeds but our motives and our opportunities as well.

God will take into consideration the struggles we have had, not the apparent victory. God knows that it is easier for some people to live a joyous, victorious life than for others. And He will take that knowledge into account. He knows that it is easier to live a happy life when all goes well than when one is afflicted as so many are. The Lord will take this into account and give a special reward to those who have apparently done the least because of the limitations of life.

Many a humble saint of God who suffered upon the bed of affliction will receive a greater reward than some flaming preacher who stirred thousands and saw countless numbers coming to Christ under his ministry. That dear soul upon the bed, whose name never made the papers, did what she could in patient suffering and prayer with the limited opportunities and talents she had, while the preacher wasted his spiritual substance in luxury and ease.

Yes, God will judge on the basis of opportunity and faithfulness, and there will be many surprises in heaven. When the rewards are given out, I expect to take a seat far behind some of you precious souls whose voices are never heard by the public.

At that day and at that reckoning, God will take into account all things. He will remember that it is easier for some to live a victorious life than for others. It is easier to live for Jesus when all is prosperous than when all is sorrow and pain.

The man who has a faithful and supportive wife may find it easier to live for Christ than the man who is married to an unbeliever. The woman who has a godly, understanding husband may find it easier to be cheerful and happy than the wife who has an unfaithful, drunken husband. The Lord will take that into account, too.

Even our dispositions will be taken into account. Some people are even-tempered. It is no effort for them to control themselves. They are "born that way" and retain that control. Others come into the world with the fiery disposition of a Peter. After they are saved, they still have that same old flesh and disposition;

and while they should have victory, no one but God knows the hard battle they wage—a battle which those of you who do not have the same temperament or disposition know nothing about.

Many people who seem to live the victorious life do not fight a battle nearly so difficult as that waged by others who are apparently defeated. I thank God that when the rewards are handed out, the Judge is going to take all this into account.

Yes, beloved, soon the Lord will come, and then we shall understand. That is what David meant when he cried out, "Hope thou in God; for I shall yet praise him." And that is the final step.

5. *Praise Him at all times.* We have a bright tomorrow. Soon the day of His coming will be here, and then we shall know as we are known: "For now we see through a glass, darkly; but then face to face: now I know in part; but then shall I know even as also I am known" (1 Corinthians 13:12).

ELEVEN

HIS GRACE IS SUFFICIENT

For our light affliction, which is but for a moment, worketh for us a far more exceeding and eternal weight of glory; while we look not at the things which are seen, but at the things which are not seen: for the things which are seen are temporal; but the things which are not seen are eternal (2 Corinthians 4:17–18).

Why are so many Christians afflicted? Why do God's people suffer? These are questions that are asked a thousand times a day by multitudes of God's dear people afflicted and smitten, suffering and languishing, bowed down with grievous burdens and heavy loads.

Suffering is not an abnormal experience among believers. Rather, the Christian who does not suffer, who does not have a thorn in the flesh, is abnormal. Jesus said, "In the world ye shall have tribulation," and in Acts we read that we "must through much tribulation enter in the kingdom of God." So let us accept the truth that being a Christian does not exempt us from affliction and suffering.

HIS GRACE IS SUFFICIENT

The Lord not only permits His children
to suffer affliction, but He also provides the
needed grace to bear whatever He may send
upon them. When Paul prayed three times to
have his thorn in the flesh removed, the Lord
answered, "My grace is sufficient for thee"
(2 Corinthians 12:9). But even beyond that, the
Lord has revealed that everything He sends
the believer is for His own glory and for the
believer's good. Everything that happens to us
has some bearing on our future glory and the
joys of heaven and eternity.

In 2 Corinthians 4:17–18 Paul gives us a
glimpse into the purposes of God in sending
afflictions upon us. Notice the words "our light
affliction." This is a remarkable statement from
the pen of Paul. When we consider what he
endured during the years after his conversion,
we wonder how the apostle could say, "our light
affliction."

From the day he was converted, Paul had
been afflicted. He had been imprisoned,
shipwrecked, beaten, scourged, maligned,
threatened, and stoned. He had known poverty,
want, and hunger; and besides the ignominy of
being rejected by his own nation and hounded

from place to place, he was afflicted with a thorn in the flesh, a messenger of Satan to buffet him. Before his life was over, he would be falsely accused, imprisoned, condemned, and finally beheaded for the cause of Christ whom he loved.

"Is this a light affliction?" we ask. "Yes," says Paul, "it is a light affliction."

None of us has suffered as Paul did, and yet how often we murmur and repine and become discouraged and blue and downhearted and feel that our lot is worse than that of anyone else on earth! It is well, therefore, for us to give heed to the words of a man who suffered greatly, and all of it for the sake of his love for the Lord Jesus Christ. "Yes," says Paul, "it is but a light affliction."

IT IS BUT FOR A MOMENT

Paul makes his statement all the more striking when he tells us that the affliction is only for a little while. He says, "Our light affliction, which is but for a moment."

As far as we can determine, Paul served the Lord Jesus for more than thirty-five years— from the day he met the Lord on the way to Damascus until the day he was executed in

Rome; and he calls those thirty-five years of suffering and affliction, of privation and starvation, of beatings and imprisonments, only a "moment."

What right have we, as believers, who have not been so faithful to or zealous for our Lord as Paul was, to expect that we shall escape these things that Paul experienced? And yet all too often we think that the pathway of the Christian should be roses and sunshine and that when we have troubles and tribulations there is something wrong. It was not thus with Paul, or Job, or David, or Isaiah, or Jeremiah, or John the Baptist, or James, or Peter, or John, or Paul.

If the Lord does not send us affliction and trials, we may well doubt whether He sees in us anything worthy of development. The more fruitful your life, the more the Lord will cultivate it, and plow it, and bestow labor upon it. No plow point ever pierces the barren desert sands; but the more productive the field, the more it is plowed.

So, too, with us. Our worth to Christ may often be measured by the trials and testings He sends upon us. Undoubtedly it was because Paul realized this that he could call his grievous troubles a "light affliction . . . for a moment."

ONLY FIRE PURIFIES

God's purpose in saving men and women is to make them, ultimately, like their Savior, the Lord Jesus Christ. John says: "Beloved, now are we the sons of God, and it doth not yet appear what we shall be: but we know that, when he shall appear, we shall be like him; for we shall see him as he is" (1 John 3:2).

God's purpose in choosing us is to make us like His Son Jesus. In Romans 8 we read: "For whom he did foreknow, he also did predestinate to be conformed to the image of his Son, that he might be the firstborn among many brethren" (Romans 8:29).

That process of making us like Jesus begins here and now. God is not going to let us be as unlike His Son as possible and then suddenly, when He comes, change us into His likeness. The Lord is busy even now seeking to make us more Christlike. And that cannot be done without suffering. The Holy Spirit tells us that even Jesus was not made perfect without suffering. Testing, trial, suffering, and chastening are God's way of purifying and cleansing and conforming His children to the image of His Son.

Suffering one, upon your bed of illness, do you realize why you are here? God is making you like His Son, and in His wise providence this is one of the ways He is accomplishing it.

NOT NOW, BUT THEN

The greatest comfort God has given to His afflicted ones is the assurance that all our suffering here below will be fully and completely and superabundantly rewarded by-and-by with a glory so great and unspeakable that the trials of this life will truly seem like light afflictions that were indeed only for a moment.

The sufferer's crown is one of the most precious crowns God will give His children. He associates suffering with a special crown of glory. James tells us: "Blessed is the man that endureth temptation: for when he is tried, he shall receive the crown of life, which the Lord hath promised to them that love him" (James 1:12).

Peter also speaks of this: "Beloved, think it not strange concerning the fiery trial which is to try you, as though some strange thing happened unto you: but rejoice, inasmuch as ye are partakers of Christ's sufferings; that, when his glory shall be revealed, ye may be glad also with exceeding joy" (1 Peter 4:12–13).

Paul assures Timothy that "if we suffer, we shall also reign with him." Oh, there is a glory for those who suffer patiently here below!

WHILE WE LOOK NOT

Paul says in our theme text: "For our light affliction, which is but for a moment, worketh for us a far more exceeding and eternal weight of glory; while we look not at the things which are seen, but at the things which are not seen: for the things which are seen are temporal; but the things which are not seen are eternal" (2 Corinthians 4:17–18).

Notice verse 18 carefully. Paul says that our afflictions seem light and brief if we look at them in the right way. While we look at them in a temporal way, only in light of the present, they are heavy and wearisome. But if we look beyond the temporal to the future, to the time of rewards, our sufferings are nothing by comparison.

Do you get the point Paul is trying to make? He says, "Interpret your trials in the light of eternity and the future glory." As we suffer, we think of what God is doing and the glory He is preparing and the rewards we shall receive for patient endurance when Jesus comes. A few years of suffering is short compared with eternity. These burdens are light in comparison with the weight of glory that shall be revealed in us. The price we pay now is nothing compared with the wealth which is awaiting us.

Look at your troubles alone, and you go down. Look at the glory ahead and realize what God in love is preparing you for, and you can still praise Him through your tears.

Jesus viewed all things in the light of eternity. The writer of Hebrews tells us: "Wherefore seeing we also are compassed about with so great a cloud of witnesses, let us lay aside every weight, and the sin which doth so easily beset us, and let us run with patience the race that is set before us, looking unto Jesus the author and finisher of our faith; who for the joy that was set before him endured the cross, despising the shame, and is set down at the right hand of the throne of God" (Hebrews 12:1–2).

Jesus suffered beating, spitting, pain, reviling, scoffing, agony, and death on the cross for the joy that was set before Him—the joy of saving others—the joy of bringing many sons and daughters to glory. As a mother bears the pain and the agony for the joy of hearing her child's cry, so Jesus suffered joyfully for our redemption. It is all in the way we look at our trials. Interpreted in terms of coming glory and eternity, they are light and "but for a moment."

Are you afflicted and suffering, precious child of God? Then remember—your Father still knows best, and He has something wonderful for you. Grapes must be crushed before wine can be made. Unless the violin string is stretched until it cries out in pain, there is no music in it. Wheat must be broken to make bread. We may not know what God is doing now, but someday we shall understand and be like Him.

May Riley Smith has written these words of comfort:

> If we could push ajar the gates of life,
> And stand within and all God's workings
>   see,
> We could interpret all this doubt and strife,
> And for each mystery could find a key!
>
> But not today. Then be content, poor heart!
> God's plans like lilies pure and white unfold;
> We must not tear the close-shut leaves
>   apart;
> Time will reveal the calyxes of gold.

And if, through patient toil, we reach the
    land
Where tired feet, with sandals loosed, may
    rest,
When we shall clearly see and understand,
I think that we will say, "God knew the
    best!"

NOTE TO THE READER

The publisher invites you to share your response to the message of this book by writing Discovery House, P.O. Box 3566, Grand Rapids, MI 49501, USA. For information about other Discovery House books, music, or DVDs, contact us at the same address or call 1–800–653–8333. Find us online at dhp.org or send e-mail to books@dhp.org.